REIMAGINE...REFRAME...RISE...

REIMAGINE
REFRAME
RISE

Defeat suicidal thoughts, re-envision the light within, embrace your purpose, and live again.

Ashlyn M. Anderson

REIMAGINE, REFRAME AND RISE: DEFEAT SUICIDAL THOUGHTS, RE-ENVISION THE LIGHT WITHIN, EMBRACE YOUR PURPOSE, AND LIVE AGAIN.

Copyright © 2025 by Ashlyn M. Anderson.

All Rights Reserved.

No part of this publication may be reproduced or transmitted in any form or by any means, including photocopying, recording, or other electronic or mechanical methods, without the Publisher's prior written permission.

Publishing services by:

The Self-Publish Connection
Kingston, Jamaica
https://theselfpublishconnection.com
IG: @theselfpublishconnection
Facebook: The Self-Publish Connection
YouTube: @theselfpublishconnection

ISBN: 978-976-655-160-5

DEDICATION

This book is dedicated to those who gave up before they even started fighting, those who believed they didn't have the strength to fight and those who gave up during the fight.

The book is also specially dedicated to those who are afraid to fight, the ones who don't believe they will ever win the fight and those who are still fighting.

Finally, to the strong ones who are always helping others along the way but forgetting they too should take care of themselves on this life journey.

TABLE OF CONTENTS

ACKNOWLEDGMENT i
INTRODUCTION iii
CHAPTER 1: MENTALLY RE-BUILD YOURSELF.. 1
CHAPTER 2: IT IS GOING TO BE OKAY 6
CHAPTER 3: HELP IS ON ITS WAY... 9
CHAPTER 4: YOU CAN SMILE AGAIN 12
CHAPTER 5: YOU ARE STRONGER THAN YOU THINK............................. 16
CHAPTER 6: CHOOSING YOU 20
CHAPTER 7: LIFE AND DEATH ARE IN THE POWER OF YOUR TONGUE....... 22
CHAPTER 8: YOU ARE WHO GOD SAYS YOU ARE 25
CHAPTER 9: THE MIND IS POWERFUL 27
CHAPTER 10: YOU ARE MORE THAN A CONQUEROR 29
CHAPTER 11: YOU CAN ONLY WIN WHEN YOU DON'T QUIT 31
CHAPTER 12: YOU ARE STRONG ENOUGH TO OVERCOME AND HEAL FROM YOUR STRUGGLES
.... 33
CHAPTER 13: PEOPLE WILL ALWAYS TALK; LET THEM 37
CHAPTER 14: PAIN IS A PART OF LIFE; DON'T LET THIS ONE CONSUME YOU 40
CHAPTER 15: SOMEONE IS WAITING ON YOUR STORY FOR THEIR SURVIVAL 42
CHAPTER 16: TAKING CARE OF YOUR MENTAL SELF 45
CHAPTER 17: BE UNSTOPPABLE AND APPRECIATE YOURSELF 48
CHAPTER 18: TAKING ACCOUNTABILITY FOR YOUR ACTIONS IS ANOTHER FACTOR IN HEALING
.... 50

- CHAPTER 19: STAY POSITIVE AND PRACTICE SELF-CARE 54
- CHAPTER 20: FACING THE TRUTH 58
- CHAPTER 21: FINDING THE GOOD IN A BAD SITUATION 61
- CHAPTER 22: GOD'S REVELATION AND TIMING 63
- CHAPTER 23: TRUSTING GOD THROUGH THE ROUGH PATCHES 65
- CHAPTER 24: YOU ARE AS GOOD AS YOUR LAST THOUGHT; ALWAYS THINK POSITIVELY 69
- CHAPTER 25: WORK AT YOUR OWN SPEED; YOUR TIME IS YOUR TIME 72
- CHAPTER 26: IF ONLY YOU COULD SEE HOW STRONG YOU ARE 75
- CHAPTER 27: WINNING THROUGH YOUR PAIN 77
- CHAPTER 28: YOU ARE A LIGHT; DON'T BE AFRAID TO SHINE 79
- CHAPTER 29: SPEAK GOOD OVER YOURSELF; YOU ARE COMING OUT 81
- CHAPTER 30: 7 TIMES RISE, 7 TIMES FALL 83
- CHAPTER 31: A GRATEFUL HEART EQUALS PEACE AND CONTENTMENT 85
- CHAPTER 32: GOD IS THE BEST COMFORTER, HEALER, AND FRIEND 87
- CHAPTER 33: PRAYER CHANGES THINGS 90
- CHAPTER 34: YOU CAN, AND YOU WILL 92
- CHAPTER 35: FORGIVE ANYWAY 94
- CHAPTER 36: YOU MATTER, AND WHERE YOU ARE GOING IS IMPORTANT 97
- CHAPTER 37: TAKE IT EASY ON YOURSELF 99
- CHAPTER 38: LIVE A LITTLE 101
- CHAPTER 39: BEAUTY IN YOUR PAIN 104
- CHAPTER 40: TIME TO ACCEPT CHANGES 107
- CHAPTER 41: I AM FREE 110
- CHAPTER 42: I AM A SURVIVOR 112
- CONCLUSION 114

ABOUT THE AUTHOR 116

ACKNOWLEDGMENT

I want to take this opportunity to express my heartfelt gratitude to those who have helped bring this book to fruition.

I would also like to thank my family and friends for their unwavering support on the journey and for being there for me when I needed a hand to hold. Your understanding and patience provided me with the safe space I needed to explore difficult moments and heal along the way. Thank you for being my sounding board and believing in the power of this work.

To my editor and publishing team, your expertise and feedback have been invaluable. Your commitment to excellence has ensured that this book reaches as many people as possible, and for that, I am immensely grateful.

Lastly, I want to acknowledge every reader who picks up this book. Your willingness to engage with difficult topics reflects a desire for understanding and growth. May you find hope, healing, and the tools you need to navigate your journey toward wellness.

INTRODUCTION

This book is an instructional guide written to encourage and help others who are struggling with the challenges of mental imbalances.

As I put this book together, I couldn't help but relive everything I had been through. Every single word of a book that I envisioned with the world in mind spoke directly to me. I couldn't help but notice how my life has changed over the years. I have grown through my own circumstances and from the experiences of others, and I have decided to become a better person to put myself in a better position.

Despite the overwhelming obstacles we all face, I realised that these issues might not have been adequately addressed by our ancestors or those closest to us to benefit their future generations. Therefore, I have decided to join the many others who are doing their best to help a nation in need.

To everyone, the strong and the not-so-strong, I want you to let this book exemplify noteworthy thoughts and words that hold the gold of knowledge, which can make you wealthy not in money but in wisdom, despite your pain. Then, use this wealth of knowledge to help create change for your children, friends, family, and the rest of the world.

It is clear that sometimes we feel like no one can relate to the struggles that we are facing, but look at it this way: the important thing is not for them to, but for you to get through whatever is constantly stealing your joy. The things that deceive your mind into believing the worst, competing every day with the strength and positivity you need to fulfil your purpose and reach your destiny.

You are strong, and you know it; you can be the best version of yourself, and you know it; you are great, and you know it, but sometimes you can't see it for yourself, especially when you are at your lowest. But I hope this book will lead you to a place of freedom where you can even help others to live again.

Don't faint on this road; don't lose hope on this journey; fight to the end. And by the end, I mean victory; and by victory, I mean reaching a point where you can see yourself not only winning but also enjoying those winnings and, in essence, sharing them with the world.

We were not created to be perfect; therefore, a perfect life was not set out for us to accomplish but for us to live each day, accepting that we are where we are because we choose not to give up. It's never easy; what you see from people declaring victory is a product of hard work, sweat, determination, sleepless nights, tears, forgiveness, and different fighting levels that most people refuse to discuss. So, you see, you are not the only one. It's about knowing where we stand on our journey and unlocking new and greater levels. We can only achieve this by closing old doors and reaching new chapters. Reaching new chapters can only be achieved by choice, and choosing to be free again can sometimes be a challenging but attainable task.

I know you are tired of hearing the words, "Suicide is not the answer, or staying depressed, deprived, and living in anxiety don't have to be the solution", but it is true. The more you believe in yourself, the sooner you will see that you have what it takes to heal and be a better version of yourself.

I was there. I was once that person who needed healing, love, and reality checks, one after another. I needed a hug, I needed a blessing, and most of all, I needed someone to take me seriously. After finally getting those things, I realised that accepting and adjusting to them wasn't easy; it took some fighting, discipline, prayers, letting go and trust. Not only trusting myself that I can do it or that I am worthy and deserving of all these things but also in at least one other person around me, even if they were only staying with me for a moment, as they poured into me, I decided not to take for granted their efforts but to use them to the best of my advantage.

My partner was the closest to me during those weakest moments, and I believed the words that flowed from his mouth. As each sound pierced my ears and heart, his resounding words —"You are strong, you are enough, you are loved, and you will be the happiest woman in the world" —echoed in my mind. Soon, I believed it and clenched each word tightly. Because I needed to hear it, I needed to read it, just as you will learn a very important lesson about your strength after reading this book.

Then, there were my friends and sisters, who were always at the other end of the line. They never grew tired of listening to and anchoring me, ensuring that I never lost sight of who I am. Every day, I would be reminded of what they had to overcome, and I would have been present throughout their most vulnerable moments.

You may ask yourself, "Why me?" Why am I in this situation? Why does this have to happen to me? Am I being forgotten? Am I the worst? Do I deserve all of this? Why did that person have to do this to me? Why can't my situation change? Why am I the way I am? Why do I feel like the only person going through all of this? Why do I have to get the worst out of life, no matter how hard I try? Why does my life seem so complicated compared to everyone else's? What have I done? What is the meaning of all of this? Why is God doing this to me? Why does it feel like my prayers are not being answered? Why can't I win? I could go on and on. The truth is, you may not find all the answers to these questions in this book, but I can assure you that what you will find is the reassurance of who you are and who you can be, and as such, it is hoped that you will find yourself back in that positive mindset where you will find your strength, and you will live again.

From my heart to yours.

Love, Ashlyn M. Anderson

REIMAGINE... REFRAME... RISE...

CHAPTER 1: MENTALLY RE-BUILD YOURSELF

- Don't stay by yourself for too long.
- Do not suppress your feelings.
- Do not live on your own conviction
- Do not keep smiling when you should be crying.
- Do not hide your trauma.
- Do not lie about how you are feeling.
- Do not pretend to be okay.
- Do not tell yourself that you are okay.
- Stop hiding your pain.
- Do not hide your frustration.
- Do not hide your feelings.
- Do not pretend you have everything under control.
- Do not play tough.
- Always start your day with positive thoughts.

Throughout my youth, I remember distancing myself from the world as I allowed external opinions to shape my thoughts and actions. After becoming an adult, I realised that no matter what we do, people will always talk, and no matter how much good a person does, how kindly we portray ourselves, or how greatly we strive, someone will always interpret it negatively. I have learned that to survive, I need to take each situation as it comes and deal with it accordingly. I started apologising to myself where necessary, ignoring what naysayers may plot or say against me, and trying my best to move on.

As a natural helper to anyone who reached out to me, there was a time when I tried to be there for just about anyone who needed my assistance. I recall one night during one of our virtual Bible studies when my pastor shared a message she had received from God for me.

She said, 'Ashlyn, God said to tell you that you cannot save everyone,' and so I realised that instead of giving all of myself, it was better to assist these people in directing all they are facing to God. But how do we direct all our problems to God and challenge ourselves to stand up against what was meant to harm us? I would start by acknowledging who God is and recognizing it as an absolute privilege to have a God whom we can call upon to rescue us whenever we need Him.

Therefore, if you are someone who suppresses your feelings, bullies yourself through your thoughts, and constantly highlights your lack of capabilities instead of working on yourself, you have already lost the race to self-perseverance and mental stability. We should not be afraid to acknowledge what we are feeling at any given moment. If you are sad, you are sad; if you are depressed, you are depressed; and if you are sick, you are sick. Those things come with life. Nevertheless, try not to accept these things so that they can be a part of you. You should only acknowledge them to identify what they are, so you can rebuke and effectively revoke these thoughts. In contrast, you seek help to diminish any form of attachment that may affect your mental well-being. Let us start with the few steps below to help ourselves out of our low-key self-destructive practices.

Do not live on your own conviction: In cases of mental imbalance, entertaining the negative thoughts that present themselves in our minds and hearts could be self-destructive. Therefore, we could consider releasing our feelings by seeking help, attending therapy, or simply speaking out to avoid keeping things inside; these are some very important ways we can approach the issue while maintaining the fight for our freedom.

Avoid smiling when you should be crying: Making merry when we feel down could harm our mental, physical, psychological and social well-being. We shouldn't tuck away our feelings as we only do so to pick it up when we are alone again. Let's be honest: how does that really make you feel?

Try not to hide your trauma: Traumatic events or experiences are real; how we respond to them can even be more traumatising. In the case of mental challenges, things could get even more disastrous if we fail to deal with our trauma in an effective way. Everyone, regardless of age group, faces traumatic situations at some point in time. However, the ability to overcome them through sharing what we are going through and accepting them helps us to conquer them. If I can do it, I am sure you can too.

Do not keep lying about how you feel: Sincerity toward our counsellors, friends, confidants, and companions is a crucial virtue to be held in high esteem. If we decide to be open and sincere about our struggles, we will realise how easily our pain can dissipate instead of being kept bottled up. Not everyone is worthy of making your business known, but you can agree that someone hears us and wants to be a part of our journey to recovery and healing. You must allow them!

By not pretending to be okay: It's important to acknowledge and express your true feelings, even if they are not optimistic. Pretending to be okay when you're not can be exhausting and prevent you from getting the support and help you need. The approach of remembering the days you thought you couldn't make it, but you did, is a good one to take. If you make it through that day, it's quite possible you can make it through hundreds more. All you have to do is try.

By not hiding one's pain: Hiding your pain can be a challenging and harmful experience, both for yourself and for your relationships with others. It may feel like it's working at first, but after a time, you will realise that carrying these heavy burdens on your own will lead to feelings of isolation, stress, and anxiety, among other things. We will carry some pain alone because that will build our character and immunity for our next chapter, but what's pain without a remedy? Seek help anyway; say something to someone; and, again, we all have our people.

By not hiding one's frustration: Hiding your frustration is harmful to you and your relationships with others. Frustration is a natural and normal human emotion, and it's perfectly okay to express it healthily and constructively. If you happen to be frustrated about a situation, always remember that there are different ways to deal with it. Discuss this with someone to explore those possibilities. You may discover a method you have never tried before.

By not hiding one's feelings: Sounds familiar, right? We want you to get it: again, suppressing your emotions can lead to a build-up of stress and anxiety, which can negatively impact your mental and physical health over time. It's important to give yourself permission to feel and express your emotions freely. Sometimes, before you know it, most of these feelings go away.

By not pretending to have everything under control: I must say this was one of my favourite things to do. I was once in a place in my life where I was always okay, but the truth is, I don't think there was ever a time when I had everything under control, and it took me a very long time to realise that. So, chances are, no one ever had everything under control. As the great Les Brown says, "We can't control life, but we can control how we react to it." As far as control is concerned, that is the primary goal we should strive for.

Do not play tough: Playing tough or trying to appear strong when you are struggling with mental health or any other problems you can't handle can affect you in a very negative way. It prevents you from getting the support and help you require to survive, leading to more problems for us.

I'm not saying it's easy to do any of these things, but it is possible.

CHAPTER 2: IT IS GOING TO BE OKAY

- Do not try to solve everything going wrong in your life by yourself.
- Stop overthinking.
- Do not be afraid to say what's bothering you.
- Do not shut out others.
- Do not think about suicide; it will not solve your problems.
- Do not hurt yourself.
- Do not think about hurting others.
- Do not refuse counselling.
- Do not think negatively.

The first time someone told me that things would be okay, I thought, how can someone look at me and judge my situation without knowing what I'm going through? Interestingly, I soon discovered that it is possible because many people have been in our current situation, or even worse circumstances, before and have overcome them. So, yes, I am here today to offer the same advice because I know you can also emerge from distress on a positive note, rise above, and win again, helping others do the same in the process. We know that the nature of doing it alone is challenging, and we often venture into trying and sometimes fail. However, every time we fail to overcome life's challenges, we should view each loss as a win, as it makes us more equipped and stronger to fight again.

Sometimes, it's easy to feel we must navigate the challenges ourselves. However, this should not be the case. As children of God, we are constantly reminded that we are never truly alone. God is always with us, guiding us and providing strength and comfort. According to Psalm 34:18, the Lord is near to the brokenhearted and rescues those who are crushed in spirit. Therefore, we should not try to solve all that is going wrong in our lives alone. God is with us and has blessed us with a community of people to help us through difficult times.

Also, Ecclesiastes 4:9–10 reminds us, "Two are better than one because they have a good return for their labour. If either of them falls, one can help the other up. But pity anyone who falls and has no one to help them up." Sometimes, reaching out to others for help can be difficult, but it can also be the most important step toward healing and restoration. We should not be afraid to ask for help when needed, whether seeking counsel from a trusted friend or consulting a professional.

"Do not be anxious about anything, but in everything, by prayer and petition, with thanksgiving, present your requests to God and the peace of God, which transcends all understanding, will guard your hearts and minds in Christ Jesus." (Philippians 4:6-7) This is another way God wants us to know we are not alone; instead of dwelling on negative thoughts and worries, He wants us to focus on the present moment and take things one step at a time. When we pray and take our worries and concerns to God, we can experience a sense of peace that surpasses all understanding. Similarly, when we overthink things, it can lead to unnecessary stress and anxiety.

It's also important to recognise that we may have underlying issues causing us distress. Rather than shutting out others, we should seek help and allow ourselves to be vulnerable. Refusing to seek help can prolong our suffering and prevent us from finding solutions to our problems.

It's essential not to be afraid to acknowledge and face what is bothering us. Instead, "Cast all your anxiety on him because he cares for you." This verse reminds us that God cares for us, and we can trust Him with our struggles. In moments of despair, it is easy to consider harming ourselves or others. However, it's important to remember that these thoughts are not from God. We should not entertain thoughts of self-harm or harm to others but instead, turn to God in prayer and seek help from professionals if needed. It's also important not to shut out others.

Having a support system and community can be important in helping us navigate through life's challenges. Romans 12:17–18 states, "Do not repay anyone evil for evil." Be careful to do what is right in everyone's eyes. If it is possible, as long as it depends on you, live in peace with everyone." This verse reminds us that choosing love and peace over hate and violence is vital and achievable.

Life can be challenging and overwhelming sometimes, but we must not face our struggles alone. It's important to seek counselling when we feel overwhelmed and struggling with negative thoughts.

CHAPTER 3: HELP IS ON ITS WAY

- Do not always blame yourself for what you are going through.
- Do not wander off.
- Avoid going to places where you can't be found.
- Do not be afraid to ask for help.
- Do not refuse help.
- Do not tell yourself that no one can help you.
- Don't go where you can't get help.
- Do not stay where you cannot get help.
- Believe that you can be helped.
- Do not think you are not able to seek help.
- Do not chase your helper away.

As I put this chapter together, I remember I sat and had a great laugh, then, suddenly bursting out into tears because, as a do-it-myself (not by choice), I found it funny that I am writing to someone about how they will get help in their trying time and at the same time couldn't help but be mesmerised about where I am at today. Truth be told, even now, I occasionally face challenges in getting help, but there are times when I do. As I work hard to stay positive and wait on God to turn things around, I know that the same God who stretched out His hands to keep me and sent His people to rescue me will surely do it again. By now, you should realise that we are in this together; the help we need is on its way, believe it. Now, waiting may not be as easy as we believe, but let us open our hearts to achieve. Here are some of the ways we can go about this.

Do not always blame yourself for what you are going through: Although taking responsibility for our actions and choices is important, it's also important to recognise that many factors resulting from our behaviours are far beyond our control.

Instead, let us Focus on identifying solutions and strategies to move forward and overcome these challenges. Remember that you are strong and resilient; you can overcome any obstacle with time and effort. Maintain focus on your goals and priorities and avoid distractions or setbacks. Maintain a clear vision of your objectives and consistently take steps towards achieving them, even if progress sometimes needs improvement. With determination and perseverance, you can stay on track and achieve success.

Avoid going to places where you cannot be easily located. Communicate your whereabouts and plans to those who need to know, and avoid isolating yourself from loved ones or your support system. Stay connected with friends, family, or colleagues, and prioritise building solid relationships and networks to help you navigate life's challenges. It is challenging to accomplish these goals alone. Still, by staying visible and accessible, you can foster trust, accountability, and a sense of belonging in both your personal and professional life.

Do not be afraid to ask for help: Asking for help is a sign of strength, not weakness, and can lead to better outcomes and faster progress toward your goals.

Don't hesitate to reach out to trusted friends, family, or professionals when you need support, guidance, or resources. There is no shame in seeking assistance to improve your well-being.

Do not refuse any help: It's vital to remain open to receiving help from others, as it can provide valuable support and aid in achieving our goals. Refusing help can limit our potential for growth and progress.

Do not tell yourself that no one can help you; believing no one can help you can result in hopelessness and isolation. It's essential to remember that resources and people can provide support and assistance when needed.

Stay where you can get help. Considering the availability of support and resources before pursuing a particular path is essential. Going somewhere without access to assistance or help can increase the likelihood of encountering obstacles and challenges that may be difficult to overcome on one's own.

Do not stay where you cannot get help; if you find yourself in a situation where you cannot receive support, it's crucial to consider whether remaining in that situation benefits your well-being. Moving on to a different environment or seeking out resources and support can help you overcome the challenges that you are facing.

Do not believe you cannot be helped: It's essential to remain open to the possibility of help and support, as it can provide valuable guidance and assistance.

Do not think you can't seek help; it is essential to understand that seeking help is a normal and necessary part of the human experience. Nobody has all the answers when some of us are travelling with the possibility that we will get there someday.

Do not chase your helper away; when receiving help, it's crucial to maintain a positive and respectful attitude toward your helper. Being grateful and receptive to their assistance can strengthen the relationship and increase the likelihood that they will continue to offer support. Conversely, being dismissive or ungrateful toward your helper can deter them, making it less likely that they will want to help you again.

CHAPTER 4: YOU CAN SMILE AGAIN

- Do not think that you don't have enough time to accomplish what you want
- You are not stupid.
- Don't think it makes no sense for you to be alive.
- Do not think you cannot make it.
- Do not tell yourself that things cannot get better.
- Do not say you have no purpose on this earth.
- Do not say that you cannot endure to the end.
- Do not give up; you have come too far to turn back now.
- Do not say you can't win
- You can smile again no matter how hard things get.
- Do not think you are crazy; you are just going through a lot.
- Do not say you cannot survive; you have the energy to do so.

Life is challenging, and we see that in every age and stage of our lives. Sometimes, we truly can't see the need to smile when everything in our world seems to be falling apart, and it looks like we can't find our way through.

As I struggled to smile, I didn't even notice how bad it was until one day, when walking through the city of my hometown, I heard a man say, "Smile nuh." It took me a while before I realised he was talking to me because I was straight-faced and completely lost in the world. After realising he was talking to me, I replied, "Yuh give mi nutthin fi smile bout", even though I knew he was only trying to cheer me up. Those times in my life looked so dark and lonely that not even the light of day and my presence in public could help me see things any better. However, I no longer share those sentiments; I am better and smiling again today. I want to add that most of our failure to smile comes from how we think about ourselves; let's try the few tips below as steps towards happiness, joy, and personal independence.

Do not think you don't have enough time to accomplish what you want; the belief that we don't have enough time can be a self-fulfilling prophecy that prevents us from achieving our goals and living an extraordinary life. By reframing our mindset and focusing on what we can accomplish within a given time frame, we can progress toward our goals and lead a more productive and meaningful life.

You are not stupid; it's important to remember that intelligence comes in many forms, and everyone has unique strengths and talents. Rather than focusing on perceived shortcomings or inadequacies, focus on your strengths and areas where you can grow and develop into a more productive individual.

Don't say it makes no sense for you to be alive; every person has inherent value and worth simply for being human. It's important to remember that our struggles and challenges do not define our worth and that every individual has the potential to lead a fulfilling and meaningful life.

Do not think you cannot make it; it's vital to cultivate a growth mindset and believe in your ability to learn, grow, and achieve your goals. We can overcome challenges and succeed personally, mentally and professionally with perseverance, dedication, and a positive attitude.

Don't tell yourself things cannot improve; it's vital to maintain a sense of hope and optimism, even in difficult times. By focusing on solutions and taking proactive steps to improve your circumstances, constantly challenge yourself by exploring the possibility of creating a positive change and moving towards a brighter future.

Do not say you have no purpose on this earth; every person has a unique purpose and contribution to make to the world. It's essential to explore our passions and interests, develop our talents, and utilize our strengths to impact the world around us positively.

Please do not say that you cannot endure to the end; it's vital to cultivate resilience and believe in our ability to overcome adversity. By focusing on our strengths, seeking support when needed, and taking small, incremental steps toward our goals, we can build our endurance and successfully face challenges.

Do not give up. You have come too far to turn back now. Staying focused on our goals and progress is more important than becoming discouraged by the challenges ahead or that have knocked us down before. By recognising our achievements and pushing forward, we can build momentum toward success and achieve our desired outcomes.

Please do not say you can't do it no matter how hard things get; believing in ourselves and our ability to overcome challenges, even when they seem insurmountable, is important. We can build our confidence and achieve success by breaking down our goals into smaller, manageable steps and focusing on progress rather than perfection.

Do not think you are crazy; you are simply going through a difficult time. Recognising that our thoughts and feelings are valid, even when struggling with difficult emotions or circumstances, is essential. By seeking support from loved ones, a therapist, or other resources, we can find healthy ways to cope and work through our challenges.

Do not say you cannot survive. You have the energy to do so; it's important to tap into our inner strength and resilience during difficult times and remember that we can overcome even the toughest challenges. By caring for ourselves physically, emotionally, and mentally, we can build our energy and endurance and find the strength to keep moving forward.

CHAPTER 5: YOU ARE STRONGER THAN YOU THINK

- Do not be afraid to protect your peace.
- Do not forget to love yourself.
- Do not be afraid to spoil yourself.
- Do not be afraid to spend on yourself.
- Do not be afraid to take a break.
- Do not say that you are not a winner.
- Do not speak bad about yourself.
- Remember to celebrate yourself.
- Force yourself to do things that make you smile.
- Do not be afraid to go out.
- Do not be afraid to put yourself first.
- Do not be afraid to listen to some good music.
- Do not be afraid to try again

There was once a time in my life when everything bothered me. Once someone hurt me, talked about me, put me down, or came up against me in any way, I would retreat into isolation and self-criticism because I must have done something to deserve such behaviour toward me. So, my immediate thought is to fix whatever that is. And yes, you got it right; that never worked because the only thing that needed fixing in me was my ability to see my strength and recognise that I don't need to blame myself for everything. Now, I couldn't give a dollar or a dime if someone wanted to talk about me. I am on my way to being me repeatedly all day, every day, because I chose to put myself first, and you can do it, too, respectfully.

Do not be afraid to protect your peace; setting boundaries and prioritising our well-being is important, even if it means saying "no" or distancing ourselves from negative influences, be it the closest person in your life. We can cultivate a sense of calm and balance by taking proactive steps to protect our peace, such as practising self-care, mindfulness, and healthy communication geared toward our well-being.

Remember to love yourself. Remember that self-love is a crucial aspect of your overall well-being; therefore, try to prioritise it daily. Treat yourself with kindness, compassion, and respect, and appreciate all that makes you unique and special.

Do not be afraid to spoil yourself. Take your time to indulge in self-care activities that bring you joy and relaxation, such as walking, reading a good book, travelling, or treating yourself to your favourite meal.

Remember that caring for yourself is essential and can improve your mental and physical health. Do not be afraid to spend on yourself; investing in yourself is a worthwhile expense that can lead to personal growth and long-term fulfilment. Whether taking a class, purchasing a new tool, or travelling to a new place, don't hesitate to spend on experiences or items that enrich your life and bring you happiness.

Do not be afraid to take a break: taking a break is an essential part of self-care, and it's vital to prioritise relaxation in your daily routine. Whether it's taking a short walk, meditating, or simply unplugging from technology, taking a break can help you recharge, reduce stress, and increase productivity.

Do not say you are not a winner: believe in yourself and your abilities, and don't let self-doubt or negative self-talk hold you back. Remember that everyone has strengths and weaknesses. Focus on your progress and growth rather than comparing yourself to others.

Do not speak poorly about yourself: when discussing yourself, be authentically yourself and appreciate your experiences and emotions. Avoid speaking negatively about others and instead focus on your thoughts, feelings, and behaviours.

Remember to celebrate yourself; acknowledging and celebrating your accomplishments can boost your self-esteem, no matter how small. Reflect on your achievements and credit yourself for your hard work and effort. Celebrating yourself can boost your self-confidence and motivate you to achieve more goals.

Force yourself to do things that make you smile and make time for activities that bring you joy and happiness, even if you don't always feel like doing them at first. Push yourself to engage in hobbies, spend time with loved ones, or explore new places that can lift your spirits and improve your overall well-being.

Engaging in activities that bring you joy can help alleviate stress and enhance your overall quality of life. Do not be afraid to step out; stepping out of your comfort zone can be intimidating at times, but it can also lead to new opportunities for growth and self-discovery. Feel free to try new things, meet new people, and explore new places; you never know what unique experiences may await you outside your door.

Do not be afraid to put yourself first; putting yourself first doesn't mean neglecting your responsibilities or ignoring the needs of others; it is simply prioritising your well-being and happiness. Set healthy boundaries, communicate your needs clearly, and don't be afraid to say "no" when necessary to prioritise your physical, emotional, and mental health. Remember, taking care of yourself first can help you be a better partner, friend, and contributor to the world.

Additionally, music can uplift your mood, reduce stress, and bring joy to your daily life. Explore different genres and artists, and listen to music that resonates with you and brings you joy. Whether dancing to your favourite song or discovering a new album, music can be a powerful tool for self-care and relaxation.

Do not be afraid to try again; if you experience setbacks or failure, it's important to keep trying and not give up. Each attempt presents an opportunity to learn and improve; persistence can ultimately lead to success.

CHAPTER 6: CHOOSING YOU

- You are brave.
- You are precious.
- You are awesome.
- You are truly unique.
- You are God's masterpiece.
- You are special.
- Believe in yourself.
- Stay composed
- Forgive yourself
- Forgive your past.
- You are progressive.
- You are chosen.
- You are royalty.
- You are a light in this world.
- Light shines within you.
- You can be successful.
- Your life can change.
- You are a fighter.
- You can start over.
- You can find hope.
- You can have joy.
- You can be made whole again.
- You are not alone.

Choosing yourself is essential to discovering your true worth and purpose in life. This is one step I found the hardest to do because being there for those I felt needed my help, even at my expense, was easier. Then, there came a time when I had to find me. Proverbs 19:21 says, "Many are the plans in a person's heart, but it is the Lord's purpose that prevails." When you choose yourself, you prioritise your needs and desires and begin living a meaningful and fulfilling life. You are not just a statistic but a unique individual who is fearfully and wonderfully made in God's image. You are not defined by your past or circumstances but by your strength and resilience. When you choose yourself, you acknowledge your power over yourself. Speak life into your dreams and aspirations, and refuse to let anyone or anything hold you back. Don't be afraid to dream big and take risks; you have the ability to make a positive impact on the world.

Choosing yourself is not selfish but an act of self-love and self-care. It allows you to show up fully and authentically in all aspects of your life for yourself. You are a light in this world, and it shines within you. So, keep shining, and never forget that you can achieve greatness.

Try making choices that align with your purpose and values; as Galatians 6:4-5 says, "Each one should test their own actions. Then they can take pride in themselves alone without comparing themselves to someone else, for each one should carry their load." Choosing yourself allows you to live an authentic and fulfilling life, free from the pressure to conform to others' expectations. So, don't be afraid to choose yourself and embrace all you are meant to be because you are a precious and awesome individual who is one in a million.

You are God's masterpiece and truly special. Believe in yourself and stay composed, even when things get tough. Remember to forgive yourself and your past, as you are a progressive person who was chosen to be royalty.

CHAPTER 7: LIFE AND DEATH ARE IN THE POWER OF YOUR TONGUE

- Speak positive words over your life.
- Not everyone will appreciate you.
- Do not think we cannot make mistakes.
- Do not think the last thing you tried was your last option.
- Do not try once, twice, or three times and think that is the end; we can always try again.
- Don't try to validate yourself, your feelings, or your opinion to please anyone.
- Do not keep thinking about your problems.
- Don't say that you're too bad for good things to come to you.
- Always believe that you can change your situation.
- You can definitely get your life back.

More than once, I have found myself in situations where I had to speak life back into all my plans: my heart, my lungs, my spirit, and my entire being. I had lost it to the point that it started affecting how I went about my day-to-day activities. I would just lay there in my living room, staring at the ceiling, either looking at what I was going through, where I was coming from, or where I should have been, and if that wasn't enough, who should have been there for me, who didn't remember me, who hurt me, and how I'm going to reach my destination, among other issues.

However, the Bible is one of the most accurate and powerful books, offering hope for the future and redemption when needed.

The power of life and death is in your tongue, and it's important to be mindful of the words you speak over your life. Proverbs 18:21 says, "The tongue has the power of life and death, and those who love it will eat its fruit." This verse emphasises the importance of being mindful of our words, as they can bring life or death to our circumstances and relationships. Your words can either build others up or tear them down, and they also have the power to shape your own thoughts and attitudes. Therefore, choose your words carefully and speak life-giving words that inspire and encourage yourself and those around you. How can we move towards speaking life into ourselves?

First, don't believe you're not special just because not everyone notices you. Not everyone needs to; you are unique and valuable just the way you are.

Second, remember that it's okay to make mistakes. Don't think that one mistake means the end of everything. Don't resort to drastic measures as if they were your last option. You can always try again and never give up.

Third, never invalidate yourself or your feelings to please anyone. You have a voice and an opinion that matters. Don't let anyone silence you.

Try not to dwell on your problems. Focus on solutions instead of issues. Don't say that you're too bad for good things to happen to you. Your situation can always change, no matter how bad it seems.

Next, don't ignore the truth that trials and difficulties can teach you valuable lessons. Endure and keep going, and you'll come out stronger on the other side. Remember, you can get your life back.

The power of life and death is in your tongue, so speak life over yourself and others, and watch how your circumstances change. You are not your past, and your mistakes do not define you. Keep pushing forward, and never give up on yourself because you can overcome any obstacle that comes your way.

CHAPTER 8: YOU ARE WHO GOD SAYS YOU ARE

- Appreciate yourself
- You can do better; you just have to try harder.
- You are not your past.
- You are not what happened to you.
- You are extraordinary.
- You are not the worst.
- You are not the worst person in your family.
- You're not the last of your friends.
- You are #1.
- You can dream big.
- You can be the start of great things.

Dear friend, remember that you are not just a random collection of atoms; you are a masterpiece carefully crafted by God Himself. He has a unique purpose and plan for your life; you are his number one priority. Don't compare yourself to others or let their negative opinions define you. You are fearfully and wonderfully made, and you have the potential to accomplish great things.

When you face challenges, remember that the power of life and death is in your tongue. Speak life over yourself and others and watch your circumstances change. Your past or mistakes do not define you, so keep pushing forward and never give up on yourself. You can overcome any obstacle that comes your way.

Believe in yourself and dream big. You have a reason to keep surviving and thriving, and it starts with appreciating the unique qualities that make you extraordinary. You are not just another face in the crowd; you are a one-of-a-kind emblem of one of God's perfect creations. Embrace your identity and know that your Creator loves and values you.

You are who God says you are. Appreciate yourself and the unique qualities that make you extraordinary. Remember that you can get your life back, no matter how difficult your circumstances may seem. You can always do better; you have to keep trying harder.

You are not the least of your friends or the worst person in your family. You are number 1 in God's eyes, which truly matters. Psalm 139:13–14 says, "For you created my inmost being you knit me together in my mother's womb. I praise you because I am fearfully and wonderfully made; your works are wonderful; I know that fully well." This verse emphasises how God created us intentionally and with great care. Use it as a reminder and thanksgiving for creating you to be special. Regardless of what others may think or say about you, you can take comfort in knowing that you are valued and loved by your Creator.

Don't be afraid to dream big. Great things can begin with you, and you have the power to make a positive impact on the world.

CHAPTER 9: THE MIND IS POWERFUL

- Do not assume that forgiveness is impossible for you.
- Do not assume that no one will trust you again.
- Do not feel that no one will love you again.
- Do not assume that no one will want to welcome you again.
- Do not assume that no one takes you seriously.
- Do not believe that you can't find anyone better.
- It's not impossible to find real, true love.
- Do not think that you are always doing something wrong.
- Do not think you are too good for something good to happen to you because anything good can happen to anybody.

The mind is a powerful tool that can shape our beliefs, behaviours, and, ultimately, our destinies. It is easy to fall into the trap of negative thinking, especially when faced with difficult situations. However, it is also important to remember that we can control our thoughts and emotions.

If you have made mistakes in the past, do not assume you cannot be forgiven. In fact, God's grace is limitless, and He forgives us no matter what we have done. Trust in His love and mercy, and allow yourself to move forward without the burden of guilt and shame. It is common to assume that no one will trust or love us again. However, this is not necessarily true. Trust and love can be regained with time and effort. We should not let our past mistakes define us but use them as opportunities for growth and learning. We can work towards rebuilding relationships and proving ourselves trustworthy and loving.

Do not believe the lie that no one will love you again or want to welcome you back into their lives. God's love for you is unconditional, and there are people in this world who will love and accept you for who you are.

Sometimes, we may feel like we are not taken seriously or cannot find someone better. Try your best not to underestimate our worth and value. We all have unique qualities and strengths that make us valuable and deserving of love and respect. We shouldn't settle for less than we deserve; having confidence in ourselves and our abilities is important.

Everyone makes mistakes, and you are no exception. But you can also grow, change, and experience blessings beyond your wildest dreams like everyone else. Trust in God's plan for your life and know that anything good can happen to anybody, including you.

CHAPTER 10: YOU ARE MORE THAN A CONQUEROR.

- Do not be afraid to speak up.
- Do not be afraid to cry out.
- Do not be afraid to stand up for yourself.
- Do not revisit your past.
- Do not think everything is your fault.
- Do not say you are a failure when you don't solve all your problems alone.
- Do not punish yourself if you are not great at everything you do.
- Do not be too down on yourself that you miss the blessing in your situation.
- Do not be ashamed of yourself.
- Do not give your situation more time than it should.
- Don't let negativity take over your thoughts or your mind.
- Do not be afraid to face your fears.
- Do not be afraid to rebrand yourself.
- It's important to embrace your emotions without fear.

In life, it's easy to feel like we're constantly battling against our circumstances, fighting to stay afloat and keep moving forward. But as children of God, we have the promise that we are more than conquerors through Christ, who loves us. This means we can come out victorious no matter what we face in life. God is always with you, guiding and protecting you. Fear of speaking up is one thing that can hold us back. We may be worried that our voice won't be heard or that we'll be judged for what we say. However, God has given each of us a unique voice and perspective, and it's essential to utilise them to impact the world positively.

It is necessary to cry out and stand up for yourself, even if it feels uncomfortable or scary. You are a child of God and worthy of respect and dignity. As Children of God, we are called to forgive ourselves and others and not hold onto bitterness or regret. You cannot change what has already happened, but you can change your perspective and how you move forward.

You are not a failure if you don't solve all your issues at once. God is there to help and provide you with the resources and support you need. You are not a failure for struggling, and it's essential not to punish yourself for not excelling at everything you do.

Do not be too hard on yourself if you miss a blessing in your situation. Sometimes blessings come unexpectedly, and it is important to trust in God's plan for your life.

Do not be ashamed of yourself, and do not give your situation more time than it should. God wants you to move forward, focusing on the present and the future. Don't let negativity take over your thoughts or your mind. Focus on the positive and trust in God's goodness and His love for you.

Don't be afraid to face your fears, and don't be afraid to rebrand yourself. You can overcome anything and do everything with God by your side. Do not be afraid to feel, for your emotions are a gift from God, and He wants you to experience them fully. Remember that you are more than a conqueror; with God's help, you can overcome any obstacle.

CHAPTER 11: YOU CAN ONLY WIN WHEN YOU DON'T QUIT

- Do not doubt yourself.
- Do not quit on yourself.
- Do not quit on your dreams.
- Do not be afraid to tell your story.
- Do not pressure yourself.
- Don't put yourself in overdrive.
- Do not say it makes no sense to try.
- Do not tell yourself that you are alone.
- Do not believe that you are dumb.
- Do not believe when other people tell you that you are dumb.
- Do not say you can't.
- Do not say you won't.
- Do not break.
- Do not be afraid to start over.

Winning requires perseverance, dedication, and a never-give-up attitude. No matter what challenges come our way, you must hold on and keep pushing forward until you get to the place you first set out to be. Doubt and fear may try to creep in, but you must stay the course. And not let anything hold us back. Additionally, we must believe in ourselves and our abilities, knowing we have what it takes to succeed.

Never quit on yourself or your dreams, even when the road ahead seems daunting. As children of God, we should continue to believe that we can overcome anything with God. We are called to trust in God's plan for our lives, and as such, we must hold fast to our faith and persevere. We are exposed to many stories in the Bible of people who faced great adversity but persevered with God's help; we can do it, too. The book of Philippians 4:13 reminds us that "we can do all things through Christ who strengthens us." When we face adversity, it's easy to get overwhelmed and feel like giving up. However, we must not let pressure overwhelm us.

We must learn to pace ourselves and not go into overdrive. Instead, we should take things one step at a time, knowing that progress takes time and effort. When you feel like quitting, remember that giving up is the only way to truly lose.

Consider your dreams as a gift from God, and accomplishing them is your gift to you. God wants to see you succeed, so seek Him, and He will make a way for you. Do not let fear keep you from telling your story and pursuing your goals; fear does nothing but cripple your ability to succeed and force you to accept failure.

Do not pressure yourself to achieve success overnight; understand and believe in the perfection of God's timing. Do not put yourself in overdrive and forget to care for your physical, emotional, and spiritual well-being. What will you gain from your results if you cannot enjoy them?

Remember to rest and recharge so you can be ready to face whatever comes your way; that's how we survive each fighting day. When others try to bring you down with their negative words and actions, do not believe them because they do not define who you are. Starting over can be daunting, but do it anyway. Letting go of the past and moving forward with hope and determination is essential. We know that God's plan for our lives is more significant than anything we could imagine. We must trust in His guidance and have faith that He will lead us to victory.

CHAPTER 12: YOU ARE STRONG ENOUGH TO OVERCOME AND HEAL FROM YOUR STRUGGLES

- Do not listen to the devil.
- Do not be afraid; it will take some time to heal.
- Do not keep yourself stuck; try to push yourself forward when you heal.
- Do not hesitate to read your Bible.
- Never think you are incapable of overcoming
- Do not say you are too weak to try.
- Do not pretend that you are strong if you are weak.
- Don't say you're not strong enough to overcome your struggles.
- Stop thinking that you are worthless.
- Do not believe that you cannot change.

Have you ever found yourself against the wall and felt like the end was near? Well, what if I told you that not even those walls of trials can withstand the strength you possess within, through Jesus Christ, and that you can do everything you set your mind to through the blood of Jesus? Yes, I know you may not even recognise it because some of you may think I'm not even a Christian, but what if I told you that because you were created by the Father himself, in His image, you can do exceedingly and abundantly above all you could ever think or imagine just like anybody else?

In October 2019, I came up against the biggest betrayal of my life; I never thought anything would separate me from the people I love.

There, I became very vulnerable, confused, and disoriented. I sought counsel from those around me, and only a few seemed to understand what I was going through, while everyone else tried to come up with ways to explain why the situation could have affected me the way it did in order to find an excuse and support their nonchalant acceptance and justification for wrongdoing and, in essence, prove that the love they have for someone is more important than good moral principle, truth and honesty, instead of seeing to it that their favourite take accountability for their actions. Much to my surprise, the people I had been there for my entire life, I had to sit and watch them be neutral as I stood aside and figure out how I would find a level ground and be normal around them as they indirectly forced me to accept their beliefs, some, in the name of Christianity. However, I tried not to let hurt come between me and anyone, and although it still did, I had to accept that people can never be me and that everyone will never think or act the same way.

During this time of enormous change and acceptance, I had to decide to stay positive, even when I wanted to stay on the side of hate and anger. I wanted to have the most positive outlook possible. It was hard, but I had a choice: choose God and resist the devil. For a moment, I knew it was going to be hard for me to resist the devil at that point because I was bitter, but I was adamant that nothing could stand in the way of my blessing or my salvation. After all, forgiveness was my only choice because I realised that no one would change their circumstances because of me, and up until now, I don't think they did.

After these episodes and moments of truth, it was time to move on, so I did. I realised that a negative approach to any situation could further erode what was left of my sanity, so I changed the narrative and began my healing process. There are always two voices; my best bet was to listen to the one who seeks to make all things better despite how I feel in the moment (the voice of the Lord) rather than the one that could stand in the way of ending the problems I had (the devil). I took some time to focus on myself and see how best I could let go of something that was only hurting me because that was the only way to get past the pain. I decided to block everyone and everything that would cause me to be stuck in the same place and prevent me from being free; you, too, can push yourself and be free.

Pushing yourself, even when you don't feel like it, may take all you have, but when the odds are against you and the world seems unfair, it's your only hope. Pushing forward is the best thing you can do. Consider these steps to overcome pain:

A little positivity and inspiration won't hurt. The Bible is a great place to turn to for finding peace. Take some time to read the Bible, pray, and seek God's face.

You are capable of overcoming obstacles; never forget that. The sooner you realise that you can take the leap of faith to secure your peace and place in your own life, the sooner you will be free from your circumstances.

You are not weak; you are strong, which means you are not too weak to try. Focusing on the things that matter to overcome your obstacles and become a better version of yourself is enough strength to go on.

During our times of finding strength, we may appear weak; embrace that and find a way to recharge, but never allow yourself to speak doubt on your journey to healing. You don't feel strong; don't say it. Just find the strength to fight on.

Thinking about or giving in to the notion that you are not worthy enough will not help you get out of the dark patch you are in. Instead, tell yourself that even though you're not at your best, where you are right now is still the best version of yourself; better versions will come with time.

Remember, the change you seek can be found deep within because no one knows you as you do; therefore, it's imperative to recognise the power of words, speak it, believe it, and it shall come to pass. We all can change; it just takes some time and dedication.

CHAPTER 13: PEOPLE WILL ALWAYS TALK; LET THEM

- Do not get even.
- Try not to react to everything you hear people say about you.
- Do not be afraid to change how you react to certain situations.
- Train yourself to react to everything positively.
- You can; don't say you can't; just try.
- Do not try to please anyone.
- You don't have to stay.

Life is good, but it will never be perfect, no matter how good we are. The last thing you want to hear is people saying things that make you feel worse, bring you down, or even bring you to the level they operate at. Often, we attempt to correct negative comments about ourselves to boost our self-esteem or justify unimportant aspects of ourselves. My advice to you is: do not waste your time; there is no need to let someone else drain your energy; march to the beat of your own drum, sway to the sound of your music, and focus on the things that benefit you because the mickle and muttering are just words; they should not stop you from going where you should be.

In my late teens, my home was situated between a group of people I now describe as my push when trying to find who I am, and I could only do that after realising that I shouldn't have let them bother me. I used to lock myself away in my room, in the four corners of my house, because I was scared to go out and face what was out there. Although I appeared to be progressing physically, my mental state remained stagnant. I became depressed and withdrawn socially and emotionally, which negatively affected how I went out into the world and dealt with good people. After realising that I wasn't the problem, I had to find ways to deal with these issues. I had to reintegrate into society, which took me some time, but I was willing to relearn, refocus, regain all that experience, and start pushing again. Imagine going back and forth about who you are just because someone has a bad opinion of you. Please remember that those who talk about you are not even fit to walk in your shoes.

So, what did I do about it? First, I stopped reacting to everything that I heard. Then, I changed my thoughts and began to live the lessons and blessings that God intended for me to receive from my trials. Who would have imagined that I could hold my head high as I passed these people on the street? Who would have thought that I could have these people speaking well about me because I decided not to challenge their beliefs and opinions? Who would have thought I could be strong enough to stand and lead in the same environment they populate? And yet, I used to think I was not worthy enough even to exist.

Imagine telling me something about myself that I already know. I once got into an altercation with a neighbour, and that is where I learned I had the most degrading nicknames. After hearing that, I paused for a second to take it in, and yes, it hurt me for a while, but when I looked in the mirror, I didn't see that about myself. So, every time I went out, I would look at myself in the mirror and make fun of the name that I was given. You are not what people say you are; all of us were created in the image and likeness of the Almighty God, and nothing that happens to you—no sickness, no accident, no incident—can change that. They say beauty is within, and it truly is. But when that beauty shines out, you will indeed see that you are a masterpiece—God's masterpiece.

Doing things that would please others was one of my downfalls. Before, I knew myself—way before I became the person I am today. I would do nothing that would hurt anybody else's feelings, and I would not say no because saying no would disappoint others, even if it meant compromising my own well-being and causing inconvenience. But after a while, I realised that it doesn't matter how much you try to please people; in the end, you will feel the aftermath of that situation. Yes, we can argue that not everyone will treat you the same, and I agree that there are still wonderful people in this world. However, trying to please everyone can drain you, hurt you, and may cause you to lose your sense of identity.

You do not have to remain in a position that is not in your best interest. Speak to God, pray about it, listen to what He says, leave the situation, and move on.

CHAPTER 14: PAIN IS A PART OF LIFE; DON'T LET THIS ONE CONSUME YOU

- Everyone doesn't have to know what you're going through.
- Do not refuse to mourn.
- It is OK to get emotional sometimes.
- You can live without those anxieties.

When we hear the word "pain," it immediately evokes a negative connotation. We feel like we cannot go on; sometimes, we feel like the world will end; interestingly, I agree. None of us want to feel pain.

The things we do or circumstances beyond our control can inflict pain on us, but what if I told you that pain sometimes causes us to evolve to a higher level? What if I told you that pain can be the root of your ultimate destination, no matter how unfair it seems or how it comes to you? What if I told you that not all pain was brought on you to hurt you, make you depressed, or stop you but to make you better? What if I told you my pain is why I am writing this book and why I am where I am? The reason I am at peace, the reason I can love again, the reason I can appreciate the things around me, the reason why I trust God more than ever before, the reason why I understand life more and more, the reason why I can love someone who has hurt me without regret, resentment, or condemnation, and the reason why I opened my eyes to see that my mercies are very new every morning.

You may think I can speak this way because I have never felt your pain, and that is true. However, it's essential to acknowledge that everyone experiences something they thought they couldn't handle. And yes, I have experienced firsthand what it means to lose someone to death. I have faced abuse of different kinds, and I have faced many things that could have caused me not to be here today. But thanks to those pains, I can speak to you, and I know that when you realise the purpose of everything that happened to you, you, too, will be able to speak someone out of their depression and into a better life.

I want you to know it will be good again tomorrow; it's okay to cry about it. It's okay to feel some way about it; it's okay to speak about it; and finally, most of all, it's okay to live again, but it's never okay to worry about it.

To my precious and wonderful men, you may be among those who let society convince you that you shouldn't experience pain. I want to tell you that it is okay to get emotional sometimes. Take a positive approach to do whatever it takes to release that pain. If it means crying behind closed doors, talking to someone you trust, seeking God, or reading your Bible, try to relieve the stress where necessary, but release it; don't hold it in. Make sure you do not harm yourself or anyone else in the process. Yes, not everyone is required to know what you are going through, but please know that you can live with and overcome those anxieties and, ultimately, overcome the pressure that puts you in such an anxious position.

At times, we tend to dwell on the past, which is already gone; we frequently focus on the future, unsure of what lies ahead or around the corner, often forgetting the present moment. Of course, as a male, you do have the right to be and act strong, but never forget or let anyone put you in the position to act like you are not human.

CHAPTER 15: SOMEONE IS WAITING ON YOUR STORY FOR THEIR SURVIVAL

- Tell your story
- Just be yourself.
- Someone is dying to hear you say, I did it; I made it through.
- Someone is going to thank you for standing up.

The perfect time to tell your story is up to you. When to tell your story, where to share it, how to convey it, or even whether to share it at all depends solely on how you feel and where you are on your healing journey. I recommend that you share your story not only because of the positive impact it will have on you, the person telling the story, but also for the people whose lives will be changed.

How does someone else understand that they can live through what they're going through if we don't speak up? Hearing what another person has been through gives us relief because, most of the time, we realise someone else is facing what we are going through or is dealing with the same issue at the moment. I am not saying that all situations are the same, but sharing your story could mean that the mere fact that one person passes through this phase indicates that there is a possibility that someone else can overcome their problems as well.

One of my friends gave me the biggest surprise of my life after I went to her about something I could no longer manage alone. After weeping bitterly one day, she said to Ashlyn, 'I'm glad you came to me because I've been going through some trying times, and I didn't know how to break it to you.' While listening to her, I started weeping again, this time not for myself but for her; it was so heartbreaking, and at that moment, her situation made me forget all about mine. We experienced a moment of both sadness and happiness, a time of pain and relief; it was one of the best conversations I've ever had with her. We felt light and free.

How often have you—or anyone else you know—been in a situation where you could have said something but didn't? Maybe because you are scared, angry, you think it's too late, because you are still hurting, or simply because you don't think it's your business to do so. After saying it, you realise that someone was there waiting to hear it. If you agree with me, knowing that you can touch someone else's life in this way is wonderful.

People will thank you for standing up for yourself because they will feel like you're standing up for them. People will thank you because, although we believe everyone should have the opportunity to share their stories, not everyone will be willing to do so; sometimes, they prefer to stay in the back and relate to your story. Instead, they will be grateful you took the initiative to share.

People are going to survive because of your story.

People are going to move on because of your story.

Your story will help people get out of certain situations.

People are going to pull strength from you because of your story.

People are going to see you because of your story.

Your story will profoundly impact the lives of your children.

Your story will transform the lives of your friends, peers, and even your own.

People will rejoice because of your story.

You may save lives with your story.

Your story may bring about a change in this very society.

You may get strength from your own story.

You may discover who you are because of your story.

You may not realise the power you have until you tell your story.

Your story has the power to let people recognise you.

With your story, you can change a nation.

Some people may never be the same again because of your story.

With your story, you may speak life into some dead situations.

You may break generational curses because of your story.

Your story has the potential to make a significant difference.

Your story can make way for your blessing.

Your story has the potential to bless others.

Your story has the potential to heal people.

Because of your story, your life may never be the same again.

CHAPTER 16: TAKING CARE OF YOUR MENTAL SELF

- Don't put anyone before your mental health.
- Stay active
- Do not deprive yourself of sleep.
- Do not abuse alcohol.
- Do not abuse drugs.
- Do not give in to your perpetrators.
- Do not deal with your perpetrators alone.
- Do not believe you are the only one going through your struggles.
- Do not be afraid to talk to your kids, parents, and guardians about what you are going through; that way, you can prevent them from going through the same thing and help you through yours.
- Remember, you have too much at stake to give up now.

Many people have mental health issues and don't even know it. We owe it to ourselves to take care of our mental health. More than anything else, being mentally stable benefits us in every way; it helps us function properly, so we must understand that removing ourselves from anything that negatively affects us is a necessary step.

The mind is important, and your whole body and spirit are healthy when your mind is healthy. Many people believe they must keep up with everything happening around them in society, but it doesn't have to be that way. I agree that we need to be aware of what's happening around us, but what if these environmental issues prevent us from living a peaceful life?

Sometimes, we go through a lot and do many things to hide it without knowing; these things become a part of us, and before we get better, we get worse. Taking care of ourselves mentally means paying special attention to how we manage problems, cope with our surroundings, and handle ourselves when things are out of our control. Sometimes, we take some simple but serious approaches such as smoking, alcohol and drug abuse to help us, but little do we know they could be harming us.

You need to ask yourself: Do I need a long-term or a short-term solution to my problem? Which solution best suits my needs? Do I need to address a new problem after I have fixed this one, or do I find a way to improve my health after going through this situation?

Dealing with the things or people that hurt us often brings us to a greater state of mental breakdown than we ever know. Every day, we have to deal with people who have hurt us, maybe because we didn't speak up, failed to disassociate ourselves, or feel we can manage in the present moment.

We have to, at some point, decide that the people who have contributed to our hurt, pain, and trauma should have no place in our lives. This is not to say that you won't forgive. But it's also fair to consider them only important to the point where they can no longer affect your peace.

It is also important to remember that at some point in our lives, everyone is going through something that is not to be taken as an excuse for another person's actions, but it is true. While we are responsible for our actions, it is also our responsibility to maintain kindness, gentleness, and meekness when dealing with situations we cannot control, such as people and their behaviour, certain incidents, and accidents that come our way.

It is also important to note that we need to release the tension from our hearts and try our hardest not to let what we are going through be at the centre of our lives. That said, try to be open about your situation that harms us daily.

Giving up should not be an option. Someone asked me a question that someone once asked them: What would you do if you had to go through a fire but then found that you began to burn? Will you turn back, knowing you'll have to enter the fire again? Or will you stop in the middle of the fire because it's too hot? Or will you go through the fire and get it over with, knowing that after the pain, you will be free? I think anyone hearing this would probably choose the latter. I'm saying you've been through too much to turn back now. You have already come a long way to giving up; just go through what you are going through. You have already experienced scorching, but it doesn't necessarily mean you are burned. You have survived many things before you can do it again. You have a source—God, who will help you through. He has given you the strength to persevere. Don't fear, and don't give up. You can make it through.

CHAPTER 17: BE UNSTOPPABLE AND APPRECIATE YOURSELF

- No one seems real, but you are one that you can trust.
- You are tired and fed up but can be okay again.
- Get well for your children.
- Get well for yourself.
- Do your best for those coming after you.
- You didn't ask for it, but you can get over it.
- You were made strong, and you were born to win.
- You can still dream.
- You can still breathe again.
- You deserve to be free.
- You can be happy again.
- Do not be afraid to restart.
- Always value yourself.
- Do not underestimate yourself.
- There will be a calm after the storm.
- Let no one out your flames.

This is likely one of the most important chapters in the book. Appreciating oneself is very important. This should have been an easy task, but due to life's events, it turns out that we have had to learn to do this repeatedly.

I've learned to appreciate myself, who I am, my sacrifices, my positive impacts, and my important contributions as I navigate life in search of future opportunities.

You may ask, how can someone who can't even think straight survive and be positive enough to appreciate who they are? The answer is simple: learning, or perhaps relearning, because you already knew how to do it. I remember my mother telling us stories about how she taught us how to read, walk, spell our names, and other basic behavioural principles that we would have needed as young children growing up. As adults, it's the same way we need to keep learning new things throughout our lives to better ourselves.

We can be unstoppable; we just need to try harder. Instead of echoing unworthy sentiments or speaking the unthinkable about our lives, we must believe we can do it. Stop thinking you don't have a voice, start winning the war against sickness, and free your family from generational curses, among other things. Manage that which we didn't expect to greet us; don't forget who and whose we are. Don't forget that we are more than conquerors through Jesus Christ.

Is it in the thought of not dreaming big, giving up our freedom to inhale and exhale freely in any space, that we lose sight of the fact that we are already free? You are already free; allow yourself to be happy, stop being afraid to restart, value yourself, and know there will always be calm after a storm.

We must be fierce enough not to let anyone put us in situations where we do not appreciate ourselves. We must face the fact that we are unstoppable, and no one can bring us down.

CHAPTER 18: TAKING ACCOUNTABILITY FOR YOUR ACTIONS IS ANOTHER FACTOR IN HEALING

- Know when you are wrong.
- It's okay to admit that you were wrong.
- Do not hesitate to apologise when you are wrong.
- Don't hesitate to seek help.
- Remember, everyone is human.
- Don't try to do what everyone else is doing.
- Do not take on more than you can handle.
- Do not be afraid to learn from your own mistakes and the experiences of others.

As I approached this heading, I decided to take a break, breathe, and look into myself. I decided to take extra precautions because there are many ways to consider how we hold ourselves accountable for our actions. We can approach this topic from various perspectives. Someone may want to consider it from a victim's perspective, an offender's perspective, or the perspective of someone on the outside looking in, or, as one could call it, a third-person point of view. But I would like you to forget about the pain, what you're going through, whether you are wrong, what you have done, and take a moment to examine yourself.

I recall one instance when an associate told me I acted as if I could never be wrong. Another individual labelled me as a narcissist, while others, in the same context, sought my immediate assistance when they needed someone to talk to, pray with, or seek advice on a difficult issue. This confusion left me unsure of where to draw boundaries. I did not know which part of me to correct; as far as I was concerned, I was a good person and could never see myself hurting others. Therefore, instead of being baffled by the different aspects of myself, I looked within, spoke to God, asked Him to cleanse the part of me that was not right and moved on. I should say that I've never discussed my feelings with anyone until today, and I'm not sure if that was the best way to deal with it. However, I can tell you that today, I'm a different person—a better one, at that.

On the contrary, from a victim's point of view, you may be wondering how I can look inside to fix myself if I am the one who is hurting and having suicidal thoughts. The answer to this may not be simple because, as the victim, you go through so much that you may not be able to think straight; try to put someone above you or your feelings, and yes, you are right; this time, you may not be the wrong one. However, this section is equally crucial for both you and the offenders. I believe that if you take the time to reflect on yourself, it will become more difficult for others to hold you accountable for actions beyond your control, I mean what they have done to you. Self-reflection can shield you from victim labelling and help you avoid self-blame when others reject your narrative. Additionally, at some point in your life, you may find yourself in a situation where you realise you were wrong, which can help you navigate interactions with others.

Know when you are wrong. This may help you protect yourself from individuals who seek to accuse you of wrongdoing and create a narrative to support their claims. It may also help you become better because you can handle different situations.

It's okay to admit that you were wrong. Yes, being the bigger person is difficult. It should not have been, but it is truly difficult for most people to be the bigger person, so yes, find the courage to look within yourself and admit that you are wrong. It can have a profound impact on your life and the lives of those around you.

Apologising when you are wrong. As Caribbean people, we make much fun out of how our parents or spouses, and, in minority cases, friends, come to us when they are wrong; most times, there is no apology. However, instead, they try to compensate by doing something for you. The truth is an apology would have been less expensive and would have taken less effort than trying to buy someone something to make you feel good. Most people often overlook the fact that accepting an apology can make us feel better, even if we can't guarantee it won't happen again, because it shows that the person has taken responsibility for their actions and is willing to make amends. But by covering it up and finding other means of soothing the pain rather than addressing the matter directly, we sometimes believe this will happen again.

There are many ways to seek help regarding accountability and determining when we are right or wrong. Even though it sounds like a simple situation, we must remain vigilant and not rule out the possibility that simple things can escalate into bigger problems. Therefore, seeking help, whether from a friend, someone in a higher position, or a professional counsellor, is critical because we cannot accomplish this alone most of the time.

Remember that everyone is human. This is not to say that we will accept everything someone has done to us, but the Bible instructs us to extend forgiveness to others, just as we expect our Father in Heaven to do. He also states that we must forgive others 70 x 7. Forgiving someone for what they have done to us may take some time, but we must remember that forgiveness is for our own benefit, not for the person's. It heals you and sets you free.

Don't try to do what everyone else does; one of my favourite quotes is: "Wrong is wrong even if everyone is doing it, and right is right even if no one is doing it." Not because it's a majority means they are right; it's okay to stand alone sometimes.

And when all is said and done, learning from your experiences or the experiences of others is of utmost importance. While unfair, we must face certain things we encounter daily and learn from them.

CHAPTER 19: STAY POSITIVE AND PRACTICE SELF-CARE

- Do not stay around people who continue to take advantage of you.
- Do not take on other people's problems when struggling with your own.
- Choose to think positively at all times.
- Do not be a people-pleaser.
- Do not pay too much attention to other people's opinions of you.
- Do not continue to listen to or believe negative people.
- Do not assume everyone will like you.
- Do not feel guilty for what someone did to you; please know it's never your fault.
- Do not give people more attention than they deserve.
- Some people won't treat you as you treat them; don't let that stop you.

Do you love yourself and take good care of your mental, physical, and emotional well-being, always prioritising your own needs? I hope you answered yes to all those questions because you might not have taken you seriously if you hadn't. You may also think you have a valid reason not to do so and may not even be aware of it.

Firstly, I want to examine why you should make every effort to care for yourself. One of the main reasons is that if you don't take care of yourself and your well-being, there is no way you can successfully take care of someone else.

How do I know this? I have exercised these attributes towards others since I was able to distinguish good from evil. Firstly, not even for myself, but on behalf of other people. You might ask yourself, "What is wrong with helping others when possible?" However, I don't want you to confuse the two; helping others along the way and putting yourself first are two distinct things.

From taking care of my younger sibling during my high school years to taking care of my baby nieces, nephews, cousins, or just about anyone in my surroundings who needed my help, to trying never to forget what someone did for me and trying to meet them at the point of their needs (which was really God's job), regardless of whether I'm capable or not. From giving a listening ear and offering solid input in every situation brought before me to assisting financially in every way possible, without regard for my own space, time, or even the slightest consideration of my own needs, all I knew was that I was being good to everyone. The adage holds true: "If you do good, good will undoubtedly follow you," which is exactly what happened. I believe that I benefited from all those years of stewardship, love, and kindness shown to me, but I have overlooked a minor detail. I put all that in front of myself and have found myself wanting in different ways I couldn't have imagined. If I had known to practice self-care properly, I could have avoided many situations and maintained a positive mindset regardless of the outcome.

In so doing, I've lost friends, relationships and myself, and if you asked me for some time, I've become entitled, withdrawn, depressed, and expecting more from people who don't even know how to give. But how can we help ourselves by preventing these losses? While the following points may not encompass every situation you encounter, we hope you will gain sufficient understanding to navigate them.

Staying around people who continue to use you. You may find this popped out at you. Still, I purposely want to tackle it first because, in my opinion, a kind and gentle heart often attracts people who don't know how to limit their unkind behaviours to a person who is constantly giving. If we can keep this kind of negativity from our space, then I believe we are at an advantage in managing even greater stress issues that present themselves daily.

Ever notice how "fix it all for others" works for other people, and when it's your turn, there's no one to be found to return the favour? Taking on other people's problems is one way we add stress and unnecessary problems to our lives. As I mentioned earlier, it is acceptable to help others, but we must be mindful of how we do it and remember that everyone needs to learn from their mistakes.

Choosing to think positively is another very important step in caring for ourselves. Remember, it's not what goes in; it's what comes out of you that matters most. That is, don't let the negativity of the people around you or the negativity of the world consume you; instead, let your positivity beautify this world.

Please first take care of yourself, love yourself, and be selfish with yourself. Know your worth, demand respect, and be patient with yourself because pleasing others will not make you look any better. Be honest with yourself; you are a great person.

People's opinion of me was the biggest blockage to seeing what the beautiful world before me has to offer. I learned the hard way: what people think is what they think, no matter what I do. It didn't work for me, and I'm sure it will not work for you either. What others say about you has nothing to do with you; stay focused on what you know about yourself and grow from there.

Another significant thing that should not have been so surprising to us is the understanding that not everyone will like you, and if they don't, they most likely won't have much good to say about you. I'm fairly certain you don't necessarily like everyone either, and yes, we can argue that you are kind and gentle to everyone, but you should never forget that you are not them.

I know some of us struggle with guilt for what others do to us. Do not let anyone make you feel guilty or responsible for what they did to you. Repeat after me,

"It's not my fault;

I did not create this situation;

I am not responsible for other people's actions towards me;

I am not delusional;

I know what I saw, how I feel, and what they did;

I am not a liar;

I am the victim, not the predator or perpetrator;

I will stand up for myself and my rights with God's help."

Walking away from people, places, and situations that no longer serve you should be a normal call to action, but sadly, it is not. Today, I pray that you find the strength and courage to avoid anything that receives too much attention, as it threatens your peace.

Finally, don't expect people to treat you as you treat them; they are usually incapable of it anyway. Don't let it stop you from doing good.

CHAPTER 20: FACING THE TRUTH

- Do not refuse apologies.
- Do not think everyone will do the right thing by you.
- Don't expect to agree with everyone.
- Do not believe other people's perspectives of you.
- Do not let anyone prevent you from living your best life.
- Do not think that people charging you are better than you; do not think that other people's opinions of you are better than your own.
- Do not think everyone is genuine.
- Try not to cut everyone out of your life; at the end of the day, we need people.
- Do not be afraid to let people go.
- Do not hold on to people who come into your life for a season.
- Not everyone will stay with you forever.

At some point in our lives, we must come to terms with the fact that we have to work with what we have; there's nothing above or below it. We must understand that there is nothing in this life that always comes easily—sometimes it's coffee, sometimes it's tea. Life is truly a roller coaster if you ask me, and we must acknowledge it as such.

If playing it safe were a person, that would be me, and I knew exactly what I wanted out of life. After high school, I had life well planned out, especially since I was responsible for myself from a very young age. I started planning for my life from an early age, envisioning what I would do as soon as I left high school and got a job. My first step was to return to school and complete some lessons, which I did. I kept my head held high. I stayed far away from boys, pregnancy, or anything that would distract me from my goals. I later became a Christian and did the right thing most of the time.

After many years, I've managed to get better jobs. Still, on the right path, I decided to start college. I tried to do everything right—by attending church, loving people, and caring for everyone—but that did not make others see me the way I truly am, the way I thought they should, or the person I know myself to be. You will never be perfect in the eyes of anyone else, but in the eyes of God, the one who created you, you are unique, special, and enough.

Not everyone will accept you; the world is big and wide. Find your corner, your person, or your circle, and when you do it, don't just stay there; learn from that environment. Learn from each journey, person, and situation to be a world changer when you move on. While you are there, here are a few things you can do:

Accept their apologies; they lighten your burdens and increase your acceptability in God's eyes, enabling you to receive forgiveness when you have an apology to give yourself.

Not everyone will do the right thing, either for you or themselves. Sometimes, they either don't know or do but refuse to improve. Either way, don't let it be a burden on your shoulders.

You can't expect everyone to agree with you. We are opinionated individuals from diverse backgrounds, with varied thoughts, different voices in our heads, and diverse mindsets; therefore, it is impossible for us to always be in sync.

Other people's perspectives of you and what you know are two different things; only what you think about yourself matters. Some people will never take the time to get to know you as a human being. Again, don't let that be a burden on your shoulders.

Don't let anyone prevent you from living your best life. You can only control what you do, so do your best and live your best because, for all we know, we only have one life to live. Live it to the fullest.

Nobody's opinion of you is better than your own; what you believe about yourself should be your top priority. You should not compromise your beliefs with those of others.

Not everyone is genuine; even we sometimes have that little moment to check ourselves. Exercise caution, as people's intentions may not always be evident or seen on their faces.

Removing everyone from your life will not help. I have said it before: sometimes you must leave some people behind. However, we must acknowledge that we cannot complete a race without encountering obstacles. Not all challenges in our lives aim to destroy us; some serve to fortify us, push us, intensify our efforts, and bring us closer to our goals.

On the contrary, do not be afraid to let people go. Even though it is not wise to cut everybody off, we must know when to let some people go their way so we can be free to continue our journey.

Do not hold on to people who come into your life for a season. The Bible tells us there is a time and place for everything underneath the sun. Everyone cannot go with us on this journey.

Not everyone will stay with you forever. Occasionally, you may find yourself abandoned; learn to be okay with that.

Do not forget that everyone is human; they are wrong, but forgive them anyway.

CHAPTER 21: FINDING THE GOOD IN A BAD SITUATION

- Not everyone is bad.
- Use every situation as a stepping stone.
- There is a blessing that comes with every misfortune.
- Do not forget to know your surroundings and those in them.
- Do not give so much of yourself to people that you lose your identity.

Indeed, we should always expect positive aspects from every situation we encounter. Constantly focusing on the negative aspects of life will never bring us comfort as a person and as a community; we should not always see the glass as half empty, but at some point, we must find the glass as half full.

I can remember a time when some of the people closest to me caused me significant pain. I knew I wanted nothing to do with these people. A very close friend, who is much older than I am, would always say to me, ' This is not the person I know,' or she would try her very best to help me see the better part of the situation. Of course, while I understood where she was coming from, I continued to maintain my stance. Until, of course, I finally saw where God was taking me. And those people were just vehicles to that destination.

I like to use Judas as an example; when I do, most people find me crazy, but instead of being the enemy of Judas, the one who betrayed our Lord and Savior, I tend to clarify his actions. We all understand that Christ came to die, and my argument is that if Judas hadn't betrayed Jesus, it would have been someone else's responsibility to help Christ fulfil His purpose. If we delve deeper into the scriptures, we'll find instances where Christ Himself has extended forgiveness. Although many may say this is not the best example, it is one of the hardest things people would have to realise, even today. Jesus had to die, and someone had to do it. I apply that to my everyday situation; someone had to move me from where I became complacent to a higher level. Jesus' death washed away all our sins despite the betrayal. I am confident you are no longer in the same position or place as before; therefore, there is truly good in every situation.

So, we can all agree that blessings come from every misfortune that happens to us in our lives. Let us try to understand our surroundings and the people around us so we don't miss those blessings. Let us try not to give so much of ourselves that we lose our identity so we may not overlook our blessings. Not everyone is bad. I know. Despite the many avoidable events that occur between humans, I continue to believe that there are still good people among us.

CHAPTER 22: GOD'S REVELATION AND TIMING

- Time and God will reveal the fake people in your life.
- Do not live your life to impress others.
- Not everyone needs to know you, but you can let them see your better side.
- There are still good people left in this world.
- People are standing in your way, but God is a deliverer.

There comes a time in your life when you have to recognise that what you are struggling to overcome will not happen until you give it to God. Fighting is good, and being strong is good, but at some point, we must let go and let God. This is simply what He is telling us to do, and although we may argue that this is not easy and may feel like it's not humanly possible if we only give it a try, we will see that, as the Bible says, everything will come together for the good of those who love God. For me, I realise that sometimes it's not that I don't want to let go, but I am just too scared. Events or situations in my life often force me to let go, and while they often turn out great in the end, they can also feel overwhelming. God knows best, and the sooner we let go and allow Him to take charge, the quicker we will see His intentions.

Sometimes, you may feel like something is wrong, but you cannot put your hands on it. Yes, time and God will reveal what you are feeling. Trust your heart and your gut. Those fake people in your life, those fake situations, those fake friends, and those fake families will all be revealed in God's timing.

Not everyone needs to know you; that, too, will be revealed in God's timing. All you have to do is live a life pleasing to God.

God is a deliverer and knows everything that happens. It doesn't matter who stands in your way; God will rescue you.

CHAPTER 23: TRUSTING GOD THROUGH THE ROUGH PATCHES

- Nothing comes easy.
- Do not think you are the only one who has it hard.
- Do not lose focus on the things that are important to you.
- Do not be afraid to take the risk of freeing yourself from your mental slavery.
- Do not be afraid to walk slowly through your pain until you heal.
- Do not hesitate to do your best, regardless of how you feel.
- Stop feeling sorry for yourself.
- Don't be afraid to be embarrassed; you'll get over it.
- Do not wait for acceptance from anyone.
- You can make a difference in someone else's life.

There is no right time, no special moment, and few ways to show people how and when to trust in God; sometimes, they must see for themselves. The truth is that all of our situations are different. We hurt differently, we believe differently, we seek differently, and we search differently. Our problems present unique challenges, making it challenging to encourage others to trust God, particularly during their darkest moments. However, given our personal experiences and the numerous unimaginable ways God has come through for us, we believe it is essential to encourage our sisters, brothers, loved ones, friends, and everyone else to trust in the power of God, regardless of what they're going through.

When discussing trust in God, I enjoy using examples. I draw most of my examples from the Bible, not because my experiences aren't relatable enough, but because this is where most of my strength originates.

Job was strong, and he had faith. However, each time the devil saw that Job wasn't giving up, he started to take more and more from Job, and we know that more things mean a lot more fighting and trusting in God for Job. But Job knew that his victory was not only dependent on God; he had to play his part, and he also knew God was always there.

Shadrach, Meshach, and Abed-nego also had a part in their victory. They knew that the kings were serious about what they wanted, but more importantly, they knew that God was serious about His glory. They contributed to the glory of God and His promise to intervene on their behalf.

David played his part. David knew that God was standing behind him the entire time, but he had to play his part in standing up in front of that giant. Him taking that step was necessary for God to work on his behalf.

You see, trusting God might not be easy, but until you learn to play your part, you will not see the outcome of what God wants to do in your life.

When you trust God, nothing seems easy, but you have to trust Him anyway.

Do not give up, do not faint on your journey, and do not stop halfway. Many people have accomplished it before. You can do it, too, and once you do, many others will realise that they can do it as well.

Do not lose focus on the things that are important to you. Ultimately, if what is important to you is not enough for you to fight to the end, no one will take you seriously.

Normalise freeing yourself from mental slavery; sometimes, it's not what we do but the thoughts that we have towards ourselves that hold us back. Sometimes, we are physically trying to get where we're going, but the mind is where most problems lie.

You will definitely go through pain. You will go through problems. It's acceptable to navigate through these situations gradually until you achieve healing. There is no rush to healing as long as you seek God's direction. You can wait for his answer; please take your time.

Regardless of how you feel, strive to do your best. Many people you see daily don't want to wake up, but they must. Many may be on the brink of giving up, but they must go on. You, too, can do your best despite your circumstances. Sometimes, if we can look inside people to see their stories, troubles, and pain, we will realise that we, too, can make it through.

Do not feel sorry for yourself. Sometimes, we feel so sad for ourselves that instead of getting out of our problems, we dig ourselves deeper into them. It happened, and you're sorry, but you must go on. They lied to you, but you have to go on. They mistreated you, but you have to go on. Time seems to be against you, but you must go on. The world may have turned its back on you, but you must persevere. Your time will come! Yes, acknowledge your mistake, but don't feel too sorry for yourself; don't let it stop you from moving forward.

You may be embarrassed by the situation, but that too shall pass. They put your life out there, and that too shall pass. They tell your story—sometimes not even the truth, but that too shall pass. We all hold secrets that we don't want others to know. It doesn't matter how they drag you; know that it too shall pass.

You may feel unacceptable to some people, but do not worry; your acceptance does not come from anyone but from the Lord.

CHAPTER 24: YOU ARE AS GOOD AS YOUR LAST THOUGHT; ALWAYS THINK POSITIVELY

- Do not assume everyone knows your story.
- Do not try to fix what you can't control.
- Do not try to think for others.
- Do not let anyone belittle you.
- Allow yourself to feel good about your accomplishments, big or small.
- You can win against temptation.
- Try your best to see how you can boost your self-esteem.

To think positively means knowing what you're seeing before you but not letting it destroy you. A friend often says to me, "I like you; I like how you are; you're always happy; you're always smiling," but little does she know that it wasn't always that way, and it wasn't easy getting here. I had to retrain my thoughts, mind, and entire posture so that I wouldn't let the things of this world affect me internally. And so, I can show what I'm feeling inside because I have not let anything on the outside affect me.

To think positively in everything I do, I have not only changed how I go about dealing with situations daily, but I've also realised that I am not changing how people react around me by shunning the very appearance of evil by either dismissing myself, dismissing their attitude towards me, or blocking out their entire existence.

I had the privilege of interacting with one of my nieces and nephews daily, and I have realised that how they see life at their age is just special. And I started to wish I was that kind of person when I was younger. I have watched them grow, so I know their struggles; I know what they have been through, but I also know that their refusal to let the circumstances of things that they cannot control around them change their inner thoughts is truly remarkable. Even though I know there are times when they feel down and feel like crying and have to face the reality of not having all that they think they should have—the things that other children have daily. They managed to work their way towards happiness and freedom, knowing they could not change what had led them to face whatever they were facing. Yes, I find their way of life intriguing, and I also find it a blessing to know that they can live the way they do.

I also believe that thinking positively involves not dwelling on what happened yesterday, not trying to figure out what's coming in the future, but living in the present moment and accepting life as it unfolds.

It is impossible to fix something we have no control over; the sooner we learn that things are just what they are, the better off we will be.

What about thinking for others? If the person didn't say it to our faces, then it doesn't exist.

There is always an adverse reaction to people who try to belittle us. First of all, we don't have to accept it; second, even if it comes, we don't have to react to it.

Take pride in your accomplishments, whether big or small. Rome was not built in one day; it took the people of Jericho seven times to walk around that wall before it could fall.

Be mindful of how you allow others to make you feel. It is your life and story, so it must be your journey and ending.

You can overcome temptation, and you can move past it positively.

Sometimes, we want to hide what happened to us on our life's journey; this is one of the worst things we can do. While I agree that you cannot disclose all the information or the things that have happened to you or that you are facing, acknowledging those setbacks on your journey is an excellent way to get by.

Continue to do everything in your power to maintain high self-esteem. Having low self-esteem kills more dreams and aspirations than you can ever imagine.

Keep a positive attitude, and remember you are who you are; you are not anyone else. You are what you are. You cannot be anyone else. Draw your strength from Jesus Christ, our Lord and Savior. Think positive. And everything else will fall into place.

CHAPTER 25: WORK AT YOUR OWN SPEED; YOUR TIME IS YOUR TIME

- Do not think everyone has the same talents.
- Do not think your talents are less important than others'.
- Do not think there is no room for improvement in your life.
- Appreciate your winnings.
- Do not be afraid to put a high value on yourself.
- Do what makes you happy.
- Allow your situation to prepare you for what's to come.
- Don't ever believe that you have no purpose at all.
- What is for you can't be for anyone else.

It can be very depressing when you are at a stage in your life, and everyone feels that you should have been further than where you are. I am here to encourage you to work at your own speed. Your timing is your timing; God's timing is God's timing; do not let anyone pressure you into believing that you are not where you are supposed to be. This pressure can be so intense that it can negatively impact you, potentially leading to feelings of depression or distress.

Everyone's alignment is different, everyone's story is different, and everyone's acceptance of grasping is different. Therefore, everyone cannot reach where they are going at the same time. You will get there when you get there, and you will pass those exams when you pass those exams. You will graduate when you graduate. You will become pregnant at the right time. You will get that job when you get it. You will achieve success when the time is right. You will get that house when you get it. You will get that car when you get that car. You will begin socialising as soon as you decide to do so. You will get that promotion when God gives it to you. You will get that higher-paying job when the time is right. You will live your best life when it's time to live your best life. You are strong, you are powerful, you are independent, you are great, you are beautiful, and you are not anyone else.

You do not have the same talents as everyone else, and even if you do, it will benefit you when it's time for your talent to manifest. All you must do is keep working hard at it.

There is always room for improvement in any situation you find yourself in. Today for them, tomorrow for you. My late sister used to tell me that everyone's 4 o'clock does not come at the same time.

Appreciate your winnings. Big or small, a win is a win. When we learn to appreciate the small wins and realise that every win is a win, then we are unstoppable.

You should place a high value on yourself because you are valuable. You're not too materialistic, and you are not thinking too big. You can achieve anything you want to achieve. You can get anywhere you want to go.

Do what makes you happy; don't do it for your peers, your teacher, your children, or the world; do it for yourself. When you are truly happy, you can make everyone around you happy.

Allow your situation to prepare you for what is to come. You are not lost but in preparation mode for your next level.

You have a purpose, you are a purpose, and you are called to fulfil those purposes. In fact, you are fulfilling many purposes right now. It's essential to remember that just because something doesn't happen during other people's time doesn't mean it's not happening for you.

Do not let anyone lead you to believe that you have no purpose because you do.

What is for you cannot be for anyone else. So, if someone thinks you are late, if you think you are late, I am here to tell you that you are not. You are on time and in the right place. You must work hard, maintain your composure, and seize every opportunity to elevate yourself. Still, you must also recognise that your current position is exactly where you should be. No one can take away what was meant for you—what everyone else is achieving—that is, for them, what you are hoping or trying to achieve will be for you.

CHAPTER 26: IF ONLY YOU COULD SEE HOW STRONG YOU ARE

- Do not be afraid; worrying will do you no good.
- Stop crying.
- Lift your head up.
- You can be delivered.
- Don't joke with your destiny.

Have you ever noticed that each time you say you cannot do something, you do it? Have you ever noticed that when you think you cannot get somewhere, you get there? That is because there is a strength within you that you may not even be aware of.

Our minds can easily deceive us. Just by thinking that we can't, but if only we knew our strength, many things that happened to us would not have manifested in us.

When I started college in 2014, my college fee was $280,000. I had no money to sign up for those courses. I went ahead and did one of those luncheons to make some money. I made a profit of $78,000, which I used to help pay my first-semester fee. I didn't know where my books would come from or all the other associated fees, including bus fares. I wasn't earning enough money to cover the amount I would have needed each month to complete my studies. But I was serious about what I wanted. For two years, I did it. I took my time, believed in my ability and succeeded with God's help.

As time went by, I learned some valuable lessons. I signed up for another school, but I had the same problem. I needed money for tuition as well. I needed money for the bus fare, which I did not see, but I have completed it; I'm a professional and owe no fees. I didn't know I could. All I knew was that I had to. Many times, I was mentally and physically drained; many times, I wanted to give up; and many times, I wondered if I would just quit. But I knew that if I quit, I would have to start over at some point, so I continued.

I worried a lot, but I realised that worrying did not help. It didn't put an extra dollar in my pocket; it didn't give me the strength to go on. It didn't motivate me at all, so I had to stop. Today, I am here to tell you that worrying will not help your situation.

Talk about crying. I often wonder if one day, when I have a better reason to cry if I will have any more tears left in my eyes. But do you know what? Crying did not help either. It made me feel better because I released something that I had been holding inside. Although it was a relief, I eventually had to stop crying.

I kept my head up through the trying times, the tough times, the bad times, the good times, and the times when I failed. Even when I couldn't see my path, I maintained my strength. Today, I want you to lift your head. You can do it, and you will.

You have the power to overcome your trauma and all your circumstances. You can smile again, be happy again, be your true self again, love again, start praying again, start living again, and start enjoying life again. Only don't quit.

CHAPTER 27: WINNING THROUGH YOUR PAIN

- Sometimes, your pain can be your gain.
- Don't be afraid to acknowledge the change in yourself, even if others don't.
- Do not compare yourself to others.
- Never forget that your best is good enough.
- Do not be afraid to take small steps.
- Do not forget that someone is waiting to see you come out of your pain.
- Do not hesitate to do exercises that build your self-esteem rather than break yourself down.
- Your past does not define your future or who you are.
- Don't forget, you can come out of your darkness into the light.
- There is joy in your problems, and you will soon see.

Did you know that you can still win even when you're not at your best and that many people you see walking around are deeply struggling inside? I know this because I do as well, and because of the stories I've heard about depression, anxiety and the thought of giving up, and also because it is in our human instinct to show a good face even though we are dying inside. Well, that's not such a bad thing, but if we continue doing it for too long, we might lose our chance to get help and freedom from our burdens.

Ultimately, we must choose to heal before moving on to any other situation.

We do it for our children, strangers, and many others, and now it is time for us to do it for ourselves. I'm not saying you'll pretend to be fine; I'm saying that even if you're not, you won't let that one thing stop you from reaching your next destination.

Instead of saying I am fine when you are not, say I am not fine, but I will be soon because I am working on myself. Even though you are not okay, make sure you see the change in yourself; that is a start.

Your best is good enough, no matter how it looks right now. You will eventually know where you are trying to reach by doing your best and keep climbing higher.

Take small steps. It is essential to recognize that you may not have the strength to endure something; therefore, taking small steps is better than not trying at all.

Just knock it over, wake up another day ready to fight again. There is joy on the other side of your pain; soon, you will find out. Think positively, and you will see the beauty of your story.

CHAPTER 28: YOU ARE A LIGHT; DON'T BE AFRAID TO SHINE

- Love starts with you.
- Peace starts with you.
- Freedom shall be your portion.
- Happiness shall be yours.
- Joy shall be yours.
- You are breaking generational curses.
- Some people are happy to have you around.

Have you ever noticed that when you enter a room with a clear and positive thought, you feel enthusiastic and ready to receive? Hence, the reception and welcome make you feel comfortable in that space. That is because you allowed yourself to be who you are, regardless of the type of people you will encounter; it's as if you just went in and owned the environment.

What if we were to operate in our true selves every day without even thinking about what someone else would say or how they would feel when we do what we are supposed to do for ourselves mentally? Don't you think people would have to appreciate our authentic selves whether they like it or not? I can attest to that because I have made that my option lately.

People will try, but unless you give them the upper hand over you, that is what it will always be, a try. That light you carry should overpower anything and everything the devil throws at you, no matter the channel he tries to use.

Do not be afraid to shine. What God calls you to do will have to come to pass if you are not afraid. In a world where darkness seems to prevail over everything else, your little light can still inspire everyone to carry on. Be the one to shine bright, so much that everyone else can see it.

Peace may no longer seem like a precious commodity, but it can still begin with you. With God in your life, you will find freedom in a world that holds us captive in many ways.

When others pretend to be happy, genuine happiness will be yours. When joy is misinterpreted, I pray you find joy every morning. Being kind can change lives; the power and strength that you walk in can break generational curses. Be a light. Do not be afraid to shine. People around you are happy to have you by their side.

CHAPTER 29: SPEAK GOOD OVER YOURSELF; YOU ARE COMING OUT

- Don't speak negatively over your life.
- You lost interest in the good things around you, but hope still exists.
- You can't focus, but that doesn't mean you are not strong.
- Your journey will reveal your strength.
- Despite rejection, you can still succeed.
- You're unhappy now, but your joy comes in the morning.
- Don't stop until you see that things are better in your life.
- Although it's challenging, you can succeed. You can get through this.
- You are not losing; you are evolving. Trust the process.
- You are bearing a lot, but things will come through for you.

You will hear many songs, read many books, and pray many prayers. You will read many poems, encounter various examples and experiences, and navigate many valleys. Still, none of those things will make you crumble if you believe in yourself, and none will manifest themselves if you learn to be good to yourself.

By speaking well of yourself, you are teaching yourself to appreciate what is good in your life and discard what is not. Speaking negatively about yourself is as if you have already accepted that you've lost. We must recognise that life and death are in the power of our tongue.

Therefore, speaking negatively about your life will do you no good. You must have hope and trust in the things around you; they usually help you pull through.

Sometimes, you may lose focus, but if you can stay positive and speak into your life, you will see that you are still strong.

Accept your journey; it will reveal your strength.

Please do not give in to rejection; it does not matter who rejected you; you can still come out on top. You may be unhappy in that present moment as you navigate through your troubles, but joy will come in the morning.

Do not stop until you see that things are better in your life. It may seem like you are not growing or winning, but at the level you are now, recognise that you are not losing; you are simply evolving.

Therefore, trust the process. You may be bearing a lot and going through hell, but you should have the strength and courage to know that things will come through for you.

CHAPTER 30: 7 TIMES RISE, 7 TIMES FALL

- Do not be afraid to rise again after every fall.
- Do not be afraid to fall more than once.
- Do not forget you have 365 days each year to make it right.
- Do not forget that moving forward is about you.
- Don't let your fear hold you back from being great.
- Don't be disappointed when you go through lonely times.
- Remember that your breakthrough could be right around the corner of you giving up.

It comforts the heart of God to know that his people know who He is and who they are in Him and are willing to get back on their feet, work on themselves, and rise again. This also means these people understand what they are up against: "They wrestle not against flesh and blood but against principalities and powers and spiritual wickedness in high places."

I am just trying to let you know that men will come against you, you will fall short in many ways, you will be plotted against, you will be lied against and lied to, and you will be crucified; you will stumble. However, you must comprehend this reality: each time you fall, you gain strength as you rise again.

Do not be afraid to rise again after such a calamity. After each fall, it is also essential for you to understand that it is okay to fall more than once.

You have ample time; remember, Rome did not come into existence overnight. Get up as much time as you fall. The beauty of getting up is that what you gain from rising again after each fall far exceeds any disappointment you may face if you haven't risen again.

The fear of not falling will not allow you to leap; don't let your fears hold you back from embarking on your journey.

Some falls may leave you alone and all by yourself, but if you open your eyes to see the good and bad in people around you, it will allow you to see your strength, among other things.

You must rise again each time you fall because your breakthrough might be right around the corner of your giving up.

CHAPTER 31: A GRATEFUL HEART EQUALS PEACE AND CONTENTMENT

- Never forget to say thanks.
- Allow your situation or circumstances to turn you into diamonds, rubies, and pearls.
- Keep the joy alive.
- Try to move forward every day.
- Enjoy your winning moments.

When all the struggle is over, you realise that a better day lies ahead. You see that God has finally made a way; there is a brighter tomorrow, the sun is shining again, and the light at the end of the tunnel is finally peeking through. You know it's time to send those praises up, for God has taken you through another season you thought you would never live through.

It is also then that you will see that God's promises are true and that your faith has indeed made you whole. Now everything is working in your favour; you're finally where you wanted to be, you're starting to get your heart's desires, your prayers are finally being answered, you're now experiencing that well-deserved joy and happiness, and your winning season is finally here. It is at this time you will come to understand what God was saying to you all along, and there was absolutely nothing for you to worry about. It is at this time we must allow ourselves to give God his deserving honour, glory, and praise, for we are at great peace, and we are an overcomer.

I understand that there may be times when it seems like your struggles will never end. With a grateful heart and a thankful soul, I want you to rest assured that you can navigate the next phase with more experience, no matter which side the coin falls on.

You will win, and when you do, remember to say thanks. Thanks to God, and thanks to the people that were there. Thanks to the situation, you are now stronger. Thanks to you, you didn't give up.

Remember never to let your situation or circumstances turn you into someone else, but let them mould you into the beautiful person that you know you are. Let it change you for the better so you can improve as you go along.

After this, let no one steal your joy; it would be a total waste of time to let someone take that freedom away from you after fighting your way out for so long.

It's also good to have a loving and forgiving heart. Yes, you didn't deserve it, but acknowledging it is even more reason to keep your heart good and pure.

You are a winner. There were many battles, but you won. They keep coming and coming, but you won. The season wasn't right, but you won and will keep winning if you see yourself as a winner.

Remember to be nice to yourself. People will see what you went through at the end of the day. Remember, there are three sides to every story. Yours, theirs, and the truth. In this case, your side is the best—the only side that matters.

You may wonder why I say you win, even now that you face so much. I am doing so because I want you to believe it. If you believe it, you will achieve it.

CHAPTER 32: GOD IS THE BEST COMFORTER, HEALER, AND FRIEND

- Do not stay away from the word of God.
- Do not feel that God cannot help you.
- Do not hesitate to read your Bible.
- Do not forget that God will never fail you.
- Do not think that God will ever stop working on your behalf.
- Do not be afraid to call on the Holy Spirit.
- Do not forget to put God in all that you do.
- Do not forget to praise God in your wilderness.
- Do not forget that God is your refuge and strength.
- Do not forget that you wrestle not against flesh and blood but against principalities, powers, and spiritual wickedness in high places.
- Remember, you shall not die but live and declare the works of the Lord.
- Do not forget to walk in power.
- Do not forget to pursue righteousness.
- Do not forget to ask God for a spirit of discernment.
- Do not hesitate to ask God to reveal people's intentions towards you.
- Do not forget to work to please God, not man.
- Give God all your burdens; it's too hard for you to carry.

One of the best moments of my life was when I realised that God was the best thing that had ever happened to me. You may be saying that it's ironic for me to say this after reading all the encouragement in this book, but I'm talking about not just hearing about Him but experiencing Him for myself.

You may hear pastors preach about Him, read about Him in the Bible or in books; you may hear about Him in songs, see Him in testimonies, and witness Him working in the lives of others. But I'm trying to describe the God you will experience for yourself. And when you have experienced Him, even though you love those songs and those books, you love to hear those stories and see the testimonies. You love to see Him working in people's lives; you will never feel complete and whole until you have experienced Him for yourself.

I have learned to stick close to Him in everything I do. I spend time in His presence through prayer, reading, and listening to His Word.

I have never doubted that He can work on my behalf; He has never failed me. I may not have gotten what I wanted when or how I wanted it. However, I can assure you that I received it at the appropriate time. Even after I received it, God never stopped working on my behalf.

Put God first in everything you do. When applying for a job, talk to God. The children are against you; talk to God. Your peers are not treating you right; talk to God. The enemy is coming up against you; talk to God. Your friends and family are against you; talk to God. As you walk out on the street, talk to God. Talk to God when driving out for work, school, the supermarket, or anywhere else. Let's talk to God about everything you do, big or small.

I praise God most of all in my wilderness. When I don't see a way, I praise God. When it looks like I cannot win, I praise God. When I start to worry, I praise God because, at the end of the day, He is my only refuge and strength, and through Him, I can receive all that I need.

I don't fight against people because I realise I don't win battles like God. God has power over your life. Declare it in your life and your situations. Declare positivity over your life and everything you're going through. Declare who God is in your life. Continue to declare and speak life into your seemingly dead situations. Learn to walk in power. Learn to walk in triumph. Learn to own what God is doing in your life.

When people look at you, they should see what God is doing for you to pursue righteousness. You may not be perfect, but the more you seek righteousness, the more you will see God's hand at work in your life.

Ask God for a spirit of discernment. It's essential to understand who is in your life, when, where, how, and why. You can only achieve success in learning these things if you possess the spirit of discernment.

Give God all your burdens; He can manage them. All you need to do is invite Him into your situation and watch Him work everything out.

CHAPTER 33: PRAYER CHANGES THINGS

- Pray for yourself.
- Pray about your situation.
- Pray without ceasing.
- Keep in mind that people are praying for you.
- Others are waiting to thank God for you.
- You will be victorious.

The thing about prayer is that you can speak, sing, cry, tell, or laugh it out. Whatever method suits you is acceptable to God. The most important thing is to make sure you pray, have faith, and believe in the one and true God. Prayer has no boundaries, no special language, and is simple and easy. You only need to open your mouth and heart. It will be answered. It doesn't take notes of your feelings, your current mood, or your current situation. Once fervent and genuine, it gets where it needs to go, to God.

You don't need to be intelligent, dress, or speak well. You don't need to have money; you don't need to be in a perfect location; you don't need to interact with any other human being; you don't need to be a special person; you don't need to do it at a certain time of day; and you don't need to use a specific platform. The most important thing is who you are praying to and saying precisely what you want.

The thing about God is that He is always there when you need Him. He is always there when you need to talk to Him; He has never left us, nor will He forsake us. He is always there to give us a second chance; He is always listening and ready to bless us. God is ready to forgive and take us back into His arms; He is close to and knows us.

Now, the thing about answered prayers is that they show up on time, don't visit the wrong address, and we can recognise the answer, and it does not shortchange us.

We only need to remember to give thanks when we get what we prayed for. Try our best to stay away from the things that God has taken us out of; never miss an opportunity to talk about what God has done for us; and never be afraid to return to Him at any time when you need Him again, even if it's for the same thing. Never stop praying when you receive what you ask of God.

God's promises are true, and He will always be there for all of us.

CHAPTER 34: YOU CAN, AND YOU WILL

- I am sorry that the devil used that person to hurt you rather than help you. You can still come out victorious.
- I am sorry that the devil used your family against you. You will be able to stand again, and you will be better.
- I'm sorry that the devil used your spouse against you. This is not the end for you.
- I'm sorry that the devil used your friends against you. They will see you on top.
- I'm sorry you had to go through all those things. You don't have to give up.
- I'm sorry you had to struggle this hard when it seemed easy for everyone else. Your winning season is on its way.
- I'm sorry that it had to be you. You can still come first.
- I'm sorry that you feel God is not hearing you. He is.
- I'm sorry you can't see God in your fight. He never lost that battle.
- I'm sorry that you feel left out. God is with you, lives within you, and loves you.
- I'm sorry you lost those who meant the most to you. It is in God's hands, and you can be strong again.

Many things happen in our lives that we cannot understand. Losing someone so innocent and dear, experiencing abuse, being used, lied to, disrespected, and receiving unfair treatment can seem like an endless struggle, among many other things that you face.

This may be an unconventional approach, but I would like to specifically apologise to those who have had to go through so many things they did not ask for. There were so many things that you knew nothing about but had to endure.

As a sister, a friend, a daughter, a cousin, a coworker, and a stranger, I sincerely want to apologise for the many unexpected experiences we all had to endure. I pray that you speak to God and trust Him so that you can move from a place of doubt to one of understanding, knowing that you will be free and feel free one day.

I'm sorry that it hurts so bad that you felt like ending your life; I'm sorry that it was so bad that all you can feel is hatred, bitterness and pain. I'm sorry that it hurt so bad that you try to heal in the worst way. I'm sorry that it hurt so badly that you think you should hurt others. I'm sorry it hurts so bad that you felt God was absent. For all the many responses that you have exploited to soothe your pain, I hope you take a step back and seek the right avenue.

For all the things you went through, please pull through.

CHAPTER 35: FORGIVE ANYWAY

- They serve you a lie but forgive.
- You were a child, but please forgive.
- You may still be a child.
- You are innocent, but forgive.
- They took your innocence but forgive anyway.
- You didn't deserve it, but forgive.
- You did everything you could but forgive.
- Yes, it's hard, but forgive.
- They didn't treat you right, but forgive.
- You deserve more, but forgive.
- It may not change the outcome for them, but forgive.
- It may not change the individual who hurt you, but for you, forgive.
- It's too much, but forgive.
- You said no, but you can still try to forgive.
- They lied but still try to forgive.
- It may not put you back together right now, but try to forgive.
- It may not close your wounds, but try forgiving.
- It may feel more painful but still try to forgive.
- You may not want to but still try to forgive.
- It may take some time, but start the process of forgiveness and forgive.

One of the most popular lines when we preach forgiveness is that forgiveness is not for the person we are forgiving but for us. While that is true, I can never understand why it is not for the other person. My question has always been: What did I do? Why did this person think I deserved what they did to me? Why should I be the one to free anyone from my heart? What does somebody else's action have to do with me? Why isn't the burden of forgiveness on the other person rather than on me? What about my apology? Why do I have to be the bigger person? And I could go on and on.

But as I questioned these things, the answers manifested themselves, and they also came to me in the form of questions: Why not you? Why do you want to stay in pain that you did not cause? Why do you want to block your blessing? Why do you want to keep hurting yourself by holding on to something the aggressor doesn't even care about? Why do you want to keep fighting your own battles? Why are you not trusting God?

How many times do we keep ourselves in bondage by believing that what we're doing to ourselves is helping us? And yes, I know it's not easy. I know that we were absolutely good to these people. You may not find a reason to let go now, but I pray for a speedy decision.

There was a time when I was going through so much that even though I knew forgiveness was right, I couldn't forgive. I knew I would heal much faster if I tried, but I could not. I surveyed my surroundings, observing that those who should have felt regret for their actions towards me were continuing with their lives. They were going their merry way, getting fat and prospering, while I was suffering and struggling to get past what they had done.

This is not to say that what you have been through or are feeling does not matter or that you will get over it easily because some of these pains are not solely emotional. But are physical, spiritual, and psychological as well, and they scar you for life. However, I want you to know that the most significant release you can give yourself and improve is to release these people.

Finally, I would like to add that forgiving people does not mean you will return to the same level with them. It doesn't mean you'll let them destroy you again. What it means is that you will love them with the love of God.

I pray for your healing in the name of Jesus.

CHAPTER 36: YOU MATTER, AND WHERE YOU ARE GOING IS IMPORTANT

- You are important.
- Love yourself.
- Let no one kill your spirit.
- Don't forget to finish.
- Don't forget to be intentional about your happiness.
- Be intentional about shaping your future.
- Time is irreplaceable. Use it wisely.
- Chase your purpose, no matter how challenging it may be.
- Do not let go of your dreams, no matter how difficult they get.
- Where there is a will, there is a way.
- Get over your fears.
- You are where you need to be.

Accepting how much we matter is one of the biggest things I have noticed. We take things for granted, especially when the odds are against us. Knowingly and sometimes unknowingly, we put people who we think are more important than ourselves before us. It may be friends, family, coworkers, people who motivate us, or even those we encounter on the street. We would rather do what others say than do what we know is right for ourselves because we hold people in higher regard than we do ourselves.

Today, I want this to be a reminder that you matter. You matter even more than those you think matter more than you. You not only matter but deserve all the good things you see around you and all you are working towards. You deserve to receive love and care in great proportion to your contributions. You deserve to have your needs met, but first, prosper and win.

Most of the time, it's not people who are not allowing these things. Still, we don't allow ourselves to accept what we know we deserve by putting ourselves down and pushing ourselves back, blocking every good thing to come, every good thing we have in front of us, and everything important to us. You are God's masterpiece, and as you look at another person, you should be able to accept and hold yourself even higher.

You are talented; accept it. You deserve everything you set your hands to; accept it. You will be a better individual; claim it and accept it.

CHAPTER 37: TAKE IT EASY ON YOURSELF

- Take it easy.
- Stop blaming yourself for everything.
- Be slow to anger.
- Bank on your stronger days.
- One day at a time is all it takes.
- This, too, shall pass.
- It's over when God says it's over.

In this chapter, I want to emphasise the importance of taking it easy on yourself. There is nothing too much you can give yourself. Take a moment to enjoy love, care, relaxation, time off, and stress-free moments away from your thoughts, the world, and the constant need to give yourself to others. I want you to normalise, give yourself all you give to others, and appreciate yourself the same way you do others. I want you to perceive yourself as the king and queen of our journey, the king and queen of the paths you choose to reach your destination, the king and queen of the challenges you face, and the king and queen of your destiny.

Of course, there will be times when you feel like you will not make it, when everything seems unfair and no one cares, but believe it or not, that's when you will need you the most.

In addition, it's essential to remember that you have a God who is always by your side, and I already know you are aware of this based on your current life circumstances. Yes, for some people, you may wonder where He is during some of the things you face, but I implore you: don't be harken by the days you think He wasn't there because you wouldn't have survived if he had not been there. Instead, try to understand that your strength and faith stem from your past challenges, which have prepared you for what is ahead.

Instead of blaming yourself for the things you could or could not control, try to put them behind you and move ahead.

Be slow to anger. Anger does nothing more than keep you bound by your pain, constantly vexing your spirit and preventing you from releasing the negativity associated with past problems, thereby blocking you from seeing what lies ahead and holding your future from you.

Remember your stronger days. I know somewhere in there you can still remember those moments when you were the motivator, the days when you were the one who spoke life into your situation, the days when the devil couldn't tempt or come close to you, or the days when calling on God Himself, you pulled yourself from some very dark times. Relive those moments, reach for those days, and pull yourself through again.

Take it one day at a time. Though we know the sooner we get past our pain, the better, there is no need to force yourself to do so. One day at a time is all it takes, and you need to let the world know and accept that.

This, too, shall pass. Many things have passed, so we must accept and grasp the narrative that if I made it through yesterday, I could also conquer today.

No, it's never over until God says it's over. Rest assured that God will only say the situation is over when you have won and learned your next lesson so that you can move forward.

CHAPTER 38: LIVE A LITTLE

- Be the person no one expects you to be.
- Change the situation; don't let it change you.
- Laugh always.
- Walkaway.
- Have fun.
- Say no.
- Celebrate yourself.
- Make time for yourself.
- Love yourself.

This section of the book is particularly significant to me and will likely be important to you as well. As I sat down to write, I couldn't forget a conversation with my mother about her past and what she had been through. Little did I know that how she lives now was a result of what she went through in her teenage years up until she became an adult. Though surprised, I still asked a few questions about how she did not let go of those times. But as she expressed to me how she manoeuvred and still managed to take care of her children, I could only utter the words, "If I were your first child, and if I had any idea that this is why you do the things you do, then I would have done everything in my power to make sure that you did not let yourself suffer; you would have had to be happy." We laughed at the end of the conversation, and I encouraged her to enjoy the rest of her life, but I meant what I said, and I will never forget that moment. I told myself that no matter what the situation was, I would live.

I will not let anything or anyone stop me from enjoying my life here on earth, and you should not either. Instead, be the person no one expects you to be. Let them judge, talk, and criticise, but at the end of the day, be happy and be you. Unapologetically.

In all honesty, nothing comes easily, so in any situation you find yourself in, whether voluntarily or involuntarily, I implore you to do your best to improve it.

Laugh always. I understand that it can be challenging to laugh when you're experiencing pain; however, if we can find one reason to laugh, we should set aside everything else and try it, as that one laugh can propel us forward and help us overcome these situations.

I practice walking away if it does not make sense. If it costs me my peace, I walk away. If it threatens my sanity, I walk away. In this context, walking away doesn't necessarily imply physical separation; however, we can mentally dissociate ourselves from certain people, spaces, or environments if they threaten our well-being. I'm not saying that we should run from everything that comes against us, but we also cannot fight against everything that comes against us.

Try to find a way to create balance in your life. Indeed, navigating through the problems you're facing can be challenging. However, make it your duty to have some fun as well.

Celebrate yourself. We cheer for people we don't know, such as celebrities and those we encounter on social media, and often forget about ourselves. You are important, so take the time to celebrate yourself as well.

A win is a win. I'm almost there; it's almost over, and very soon, it can all be considered a win. Start celebrating early.

And in the process, make time for yourself. We often reach out to everyone around us while making excuses for ourselves. There is time for work, the kids, friends, study, and school, but we refuse to give ourselves a little time to relax.

Finally, in this chapter, after praying in the morning, ask yourself, "What will I do special for myself today?" and do it.

CHAPTER 39: BEAUTY IN YOUR PAIN

- Your tears will allow you to appreciate joy.
- Your pain will allow you to appreciate happiness.
- Your rainy days will make you appreciate sunny days.
- Your broken heart will allow you to appreciate love more deeply.
- Lies will allow you to appreciate your truth.
- Ingratitude will allow you to appreciate your hard work.

There were many instances in my life where I tried to motivate myself while going through something and continued to say, "There will be a light at the end of the tunnel." Or I would say that there is a greater reward for every situation. While that is true, and while you're going through your pain and your struggles, it is hard to believe it.

Finding beauty in one's pain can be deeply complex and personal throughout our fight to stay resilient and motivated, and depending on one's circumstances, it isn't easy.

While growing up, I would only see what was happening in the world by attending school or watching television. There was not much at my disposal because the community was located in a rural area. Finding answers to what I needed to know by observing what I saw around me was the best of situations, but it was what I knew.

As I grew older, I told myself what I saw around me would not be my reality. Later, as life changed and I moved to another location, I learned a bit more about what to expect in life.

As I matured, I realised that everything would never be the same, and I would not react to situations in the same way. I had to learn to accept the necessity of believing in myself and that growth comes with change. With those changes, you evolve, and evolving comes with transformation, as well as resisting anything that threatens who you are and what God wants you to become. I learned from my difficulties that challenges are necessary for my personal growth and development, allowing me to gain wisdom.

These challenges taught me that no matter my insecurities, the condemnation, the disrespect, failures, or misguided steps, there is beauty in my pain. I am now able to appreciate what this world throws at me.

My tears no longer allow me to feel victimised, but they're now a source of my appreciation for the joy that I have been able to give to this world.

In my pain, I never again allowed myself to hate or curse the reason for what I felt I didn't deserve, but now I'm more appreciative of happiness, both what I can give and what comes to me.

My rainy days, which I thought would never be over, give the sunny days more meaning.

The broken heart that lets me accept the world for what it is makes me appreciate love even more.

The lies told to and about me have made me realise how powerful my truth is.

The ungratefulness that left me feeling unappreciated, forgotten, and undermined has taught me to appreciate my work and what I offer, and still have to offer, to the wider world.

Remember, in this troubled world, your environment is the potter; you are the clay. Let it mould you into someone beautiful.

CHAPTER 40: TIME TO ACCEPT CHANGES

- Be ready for life changes.
- Embrace those changes.
- Embrace the opportunity that comes with change.
- Be grateful for the strength you gained in the process.
- Look back only for motivation.
- Move forward only when you are ready.
- Let the past be the past.
- Let your experience be your guidance and source of strength.

One of the most important aspects of our lives is what we fear most: changes, even though we don't realise that we do this daily.

Every day, we change something about ourselves without even realising it. After we were born, we had to make some changes to grow. We started out creeping, and then we knew we had to walk. We changed teeth. We transition from a baby's physical appearance to that of an adult and continue to change our educational institutions. We change shoe and clothing sizes. We change what we like and how we look, but as soon as we are faced with life-altering changes that benefit our well-being, we feel as though it ought not to have happened. However, we often fail to realise that we are susceptible to change from birth.

As this book aims to help you accept that you don't have to live a life based on what you've been through, there are some changes that we are slow to accept, recognising that we need to grow. The problem is, the longer we take to admit that we are not the same person that people see us to be, the longer we will take to see our true selves and the more difficult it will be for us to know our power, fulfil our purpose, and truly accept ourselves for whom God made us to be.

It is for that reason. I felt compelled to pen this book. I was stuck believing I was that same young girl who grew up loving, kind, patient, forgiving, helpful, forgetting about yesterday, focusing on the future, sharing, and standing up for what I knew was right. Funny enough, I believed this was who we were supposed to be until I received a wake-up call: not everyone wants these things, and not everyone deserves them from me. This realisation changed me.

After learning my lessons, I still believe I am that same wonderful individual, pursuing the purpose that God has sent me here to fulfil, only that I am doing things differently.

I now assess my environment, the people, and the situation. After doing so, I provided what was necessary to fulfil whatever obligation at that moment and gave each person what they deserved. This helped me grow into the person I am today, both personally and professionally, spiritually, financially, and in my career and beliefs.

It has helped me discover the truth about myself, my surroundings, my family, my friends, and the world. I have accepted the good and the bad that comes with it. I have gained more courage to venture into the unknown, overcoming the fear of triggering or losing myself in the process.

I now understand that most of what has happened to me, especially from people I love, is that it wasn't about me but rather a result of who they are. I have learned to identify how I have caused myself to be unable to accept certain changes in the past, now finding better ways of living and leading a more accepting and comfortable life.

The changes associated with life can be more accepted if we learn to be ready. Once we understand the inevitability of life's changes, we will be considered ready and accepting of these changes. Regardless of who they are, we must strive to accept them, lead a more fulfilling life, and relinquish our fear of the past, the present, and the future.

We must also embrace opportunities, such as growth, strength, empowerment, and experience, that come with these changes.

Although we must remember where we are coming from, we must keep our heads steadfast to where we are going and only look back for motivation.

It is no secret that moving on is essential, but in the same breath, we must understand that we shouldn't feel compelled to move forward if we aren't ready to do so. Try moving in a way that is correct and fair. Not in doubt or holding back. Move forward only when you are ready.

Accept the changes. Accept the responsibilities that come with these changes. Take the lessons and accept the duties that come with them, but remember to let the past be in the past.

Let your experience be your guidance and source of strength. One thing I have made sure not to forget is to remain strong after I have passed certain milestones in my life. Understanding my strength also means allowing whatever has happened to be a source of light and guidance for my next move.

CHAPTER 41: I AM FREE

- I am free to be myself.
- I'm free to love myself.
- Free to accept challenges and changes.
- Free to move forward.
- I am free to start winning again.
- Free from stress, depression, pain, anxiety, and suicidal thoughts.
- I'm ready for the world again.
- Ready for a new journey.
- Ready to turn new pages.
- Ready to lead.
- Ready to learn again.

Notice how, when someone has won a battle, they will raise their hands and accept their victory with joy and pride. Or when something is over, how happy you feel, just like the birds in the air prancing around?

Do you notice how different you feel or how beautiful you look now that your face has lit up and taken on a fresh look as you start thinking more positively and doing things you love? Then people start seeing you differently, talking about your weight and how your features have changed, simply because you have decided to make positive changes in your life.

What about the times when you have stepped out of darkness and into light, from the comfort of the walls of your bedroom, from alcohol or smoking, or from crying and fear? Consider how that made you feel.

Yes, you can be free. You have a right to be free. Free to be yourself, free to love yourself, free to accept challenges and changes, free to move forward, free to start over, free to win again. Free from stress, depression, pain, anxiety, and suicidal thoughts, Ready for the world again, ready for a new journey, ready to turn new pages, ready to lead, ready to learn again, ready to live again.

When free, let no one take you back to that place of darkness, sadness, unhealed moments, fearfulness, and insecurities.

CHAPTER 42: I AM A SURVIVOR

- I have made it.
- I did it.
- I am free.
- I survived it.

Sadly, many people have not reached this far to echo these words, but you have, and that's why it's essential for you to be excited about who you are and to thank God for where you come from.

Indeed, you have made it through. You have jumped over the hurdles even when you felt like you couldn't; you have stayed on track in the game and the course. You cried, but you did not give up. Many thoughts were going through your mind, but you decided to keep going. Obstacles came, but you didn't fail. You see darkness; you feel the rain, but somehow, you know you will be strong again. You have prayed and talked to God; now that you are better, you have seen the worst. You felt like you were going to die, but you held on. The way was dark, and the journey was rough, but you knew you would be victorious.

You are a survivor; victory is yours; you are a winner.

As I reached the end of this book, I took my first and longest break from work, so I went home to see some of my family members whom I hadn't seen in a very long time. Upon visiting a senior family member, one of my father's cousins, she held me in her arms, hugging me for a moment. We talked long about not seeing each other in a while. I felt great and at peace.

I remember her saying, "I miss my Ashlyn, my little Ashlyn, who used to walk away when there were disagreements to avoid confrontation with anyone. I remember saying to her, I'm not like that anymore; I'm standing up for myself now.

That moment brought back many memories, and I realised I had come a long way. I'm no longer a victim; I'm strong, resilient, determined, and powerful. I have also come to realise that those years of trauma and mistreatment are where most of my struggles lie. Still, now I can say I have made it: no more feeling sorry for myself, no more doubting myself, no more feeling of entitlement that anyone must treat me well because I treat myself well, no more fighting because I know it's not worth it, no more overexposing myself to people or situations that don't value my presence, no more feeling of anxiety, no more belittling myself because of what happened in the past. Now, I embrace a new day, new chapters, a new opportunity, and a new me. The person who, together with God Almighty, has survived it all. I am that person; that person is me. You can be that person, and that person can be you.

CONCLUSION

Sharing a portion of my life with you has compelled me to reflect deeply on myself, and I never anticipated the significant progress I've made. But I am here, and I realise that I know how to be thankful to God for His grace and mercy and for all He has done and continues to do in my life.

One of the biggest challenges I've faced since deciding to publish this book is the fear that I might be unable to connect with readers and truly understand their underlying issues. Secondly, I worry about failing to connect with someone who is struggling and desperately needs support; thirdly, I worry about the potential misinterpretation of this book, which could lead to any harm to the reader. I sincerely hope that none of these issues arise and that the book achieves its intended purpose.

This book is about finding yourself back on your feet again, realising and using your strength, igniting the power you already possess, digging deep within, and utilising your abilities to walk in the favour God has bestowed upon you.

I pray that in your situation, you will find help, express your feelings, and have the courage to rediscover yourself.

One of the easiest ways to mask your feelings is by always smiling and toughening up to seem strong. We don't talk about our distress; we stay scarce and are always okay. This type of behaviour got me helping people out with their problems while facing mine and getting through life, winning short terms for years until I couldn't fight it anymore, so instead of knocking down the small barriers and facing the fact that I am hurting and masking it all until bigger battles came.

I couldn't deal with them because I didn't learn from the small ones. Instead, I told myself I was okay, too much to my disadvantage, but that wasn't true. Yet, I continued to assist others, checking in on them, praying for them, and functioning so that no one would even think to ask me how I was doing. Even if they did, I would say I was okay, which was my favourite answer. Therefore, I was unable to get any help and didn't seek any.

I believed that by behaving toughly, I would be able to get over it. So, there I was, brimming with self-satisfaction, donning my big girl pants, persevering day after day, and achieving success in every aspect of my life until I suddenly began to crumble. I have seen people like myself play tough all the time. We act as masters of many things, but do we have to? Does it always benefit us? My answer is that we should not have to. We should understand that it is okay not to be okay. It's okay to say I'm going through something and can no longer manage.

Let's discuss the fact that we often don't even seek help. First, we are ashamed of what we are going through and the criticism from people, and we are afraid of looking weak.

After reading this book, I hope you will resist the temptation to avoid seeking help when necessary.

I pray that we will all be brave and strong enough to heal from anything holding us back and putting us in the mental state we often find ourselves in.

ABOUT THE AUTHOR

Ashlyn M. Anderson is an entrepreneur and the visionary behind **A'LYNZ Christian Magazine** and **A'LYNZ Organic**, where she serves as Creator, Owner, and CEO. With a background in Media and Communication and an Associate Degree in Video Production, Ashlyn brings her skills as a writer, producer, editor, photographer, and videographer to life, backed by over three years of experience. She produced video ads and other creative content, as well as an internship as a producer.

A proud Jamaican and skilled administrator, Ashlyn hails from the close-knit community of Hunts Pen District in May Pen, Clarendon, and later moved to New Bowens, which she still fondly calls home. Her upbringing inspires her creativity and passion for storytelling.

This debut book marks an exciting milestone in Ashlyn's writing journey. A Child of God who cherishes her faith, Ashlyn is known for her radiant smile and ability to find joy in quiet moments at home and occasional adventures. Although she describes herself as an introvert, she fully embraces life.

Ashlyn's work reflects her heart for faith, family, and entrepreneurship, and she looks forward to inspiring readers with her story.

Follow Ashlyn on Social Media:

INSTAGRAM

@i.am.ashlyn_anderson

@alynzchristianmagazine

@alynz_organics

FACEBOOK

@Ashlyn Anderson

@Alynz Christian Magazine Lessons

@Living by His Words, Daily Bible Lessons and More

@ A'lynz Organics

Website: www.alynzchristianmagazineja.com

Email: info@alynzchristianmagazineja.com

Made in the USA
Columbia, SC
08 June 2025